Corporations and Partnerships in Poland

Corporations and Partnerships in Poland

Second Edition

Eligiusz Jerzy Krześniak

This book was originally published as a monograph in the International Encyclopaedia of Laws/Corporations and Partnerships.

Founding Editor: Roger Blanpain
General Editor: Frank Hendrickx
Volume Editors: Koen Geens

Wolters Kluwer

Published by:
Kluwer Law International B.V.
PO Box 316
2400 AH Alphen aan den Rijn
The Netherlands
E-mail: lrs-sales@wolterskluwer.com
Website: www.wolterskluwer.com/en/solutions/kluwerlawinternational

Sold and distributed by:
Wolters Kluwer Legal & Regulatory U.S.
920 Links Avenue
Landisville, PA 17538
United States of America
E-mail: customer.service@wolterskluwer.com

ISBN 978-94-035-3248-6

e-Book: ISBN 978-94-035-3258-5
web-PDF: ISBN 978-94-035-3268-4

The Author

Eligiusz Jerzy Krześniak, Professor of the Faculty of Law and Administration at the Łazarski University in Warsaw, Poland, where he holds the chair of the Commercial Law Department. Managing partner of the Polish Office of the global law firm Squire Patton Boggs. Member of the Board of the Polish Association of Legal Employers. Chairman of the Polish Arbitration Association and one of Poland's highly regarded arbitration specialists. His experience includes acting in proceedings under the UNCITRAL, ICC, SCC, CAS, KIG and Lewiatan Rules, as well as in ad hoc arbitrations.

Many of his papers on Polish, German and American commercial and sports law have been published in recognized journals. He has authored and coauthored several legal monographs and books on various legal issues in the realm of commercial and sports law.

The author has served as chairman and deputy chairman of some of the largest Polish companies listed on the Warsaw Stock Exchange. For years, he has been highly recommended as a leading lawyer in Poland, including in the Chambers Europe and Legal 500 rankings.

The Author

Table of Contents

List of Abbreviations

CCCP	Code of Commercial Companies and Partnerships
CIT	Corporate Income Tax
CPC	Civil Procedures Code
GDP	Gross Domestic Product
ICTs	Information and Communication Technologies
IPO	Initial Public Offering
MAR Regulation	Regulation (EU) No. 596/2014 of the European Parliament and of the Council of April 16, 2014 on market abuse and repealing Directive 2003/6/EC of the European Parliament and of the Council and Commission Directives 2003/124/EC, 2003/125/EC and 2004/72/EC (Market Abuse Regulation)
PCC	Polish Civil Code
PIL	Private International Law
PSA	Simple Joint-Stock Company (Prosta Spółka Akcyjna)
VAT	Value Added Tax

Magazines and Publications

GP	Gazeta Prawna
MoP	Monitor Prawniczy
MPH	Monitor Prawa Handlowego
Pal.	Palestra
PPH	Przegląd Prawa Handlowego
Pr. Spół.	Prawo Spółek
PS	Przegląd Sądowy
Rej.	Rejent
RPEiS	Ruch Prawniczy, Ekonomiczny i Socjologiczny

List of Abbreviations

Preface

One does not need commercial companies without a market economy. Nor does one need commercial law departments at universities if all that can be taught there would be based on history books. Market economy did not exist in Poland until 1989—at least not officially. Therefore, a mere three decades ago—give or take—Polish commercial law was rather taught as part of the law history curriculum, discussing the 1935 Commercial Code—which was a modern statute when first enacted—though, at the time, it had long been largely a dead letter. The economic transformation of the 1990s meant a necessary crash course in market economy—also for lawyers. It was then that the capital markets foundations were laid. Initially, we also used the prosthetic in the form of the pre-war Commercial Code—again in good graces and in effect. However, a fundamental change did not occur until 2000, when the Commercial Companies Code was signed into law. It was a cutting-edge statute, comprehensively regulating all matters related to commercial companies, adopted almost unanimously by the Parliament—otherwise, greatly politically divided. The new law was revolutionary—albeit well thought over and anticipated. Apart from regulating the existing forms of companies, it also introduced two new ones—a limited liability partnership and a partnership limited by shares—it enabled merging, dividing and transforming companies to a significant extent, and—finally—it regulated holding relations. The law had functioned essentially without any major amendments for nearly two decades and it had proved itself well in practical terms. Only in 2021 did another form of company appear—a simple public limited company, despite general resentment—might we add—of the good part of the Polish lawyer-scholar circles in the realm of commercial law. Legislative work on further changes—this time regarding regulating groups of companies—is currently underway and at the pivotal stage. Hence, the Polish commercial law is alive and shipshape.

General Introduction

§1. General Background of the Country

I. Geography

1. Poland is located in Central Europe, on the Baltic coast. It is a country of largely lowlands, with a mountain belt in the south. Poland covers an area of 322,575 km^2. In Europe, Poland is in ninth place in terms of surface area, after Russia, Ukraine, France, Spain, Sweden, Germany, Finland and Norway.

2. Poland shares borders with seven countries, namely Germany, Czech Republic, Slovakia, Ukraine, Belarus, Lithuania and Russia (Kaliningrad Oblast, which is an enclave of Russia).

3. The inland border is 2,071 km long, while the coast has a length of 440 km.

II. Cultural Composition

4. Poland is an ethnically homogeneous country. Over 97% of the people declare they have Polish nationality.

5. The language spoken in Poland is Polish, which is a Slavic language. The mother tongue of some Poles is Kashub. The official language in Poland is Polish, while the law guarantees national minorities the right to use their own languages. German, Kashub, Lithuanian and Belarusian are used as official auxiliary languages in twenty-one municipalities.

6. Immigrants from Ukraine have been settling in their masses in Poland in the last few years.

7. The largest religious community in Poland is the Catholic Church, to which around 33,500,000 people belong. This means that 87% of Poland's inhabitants are baptized into the Roman Catholic Church. About 93% of the population consider themselves to be Catholics (self-declaration of Public Opinion Research Center (Centrum Badania Opinii Społecznej (CBOS)) respondents from 2012). However, it arises from the data that far fewer people are regular churchgoers in Poland, i.e., around 40% of all Catholics. This is still the highest index in Europe after Malta.

8. Orthodox communities have over 500,000 followers. In turn, around 150,000 followers admit to being Protestants.

9. Poland is considered by the United Nations as a very highly developed country because of the Human Development Index (HDI), which takes into account factors such as life expectancy, average length of education and expected duration of education of children of school age, as well as gross domestic product (GDP) per capita at purchasing power parity.

III. Political System

10. Poland is a parliamentary republic with a parliamentary cabinet system based on a tripartite division of powers.

11. The most important act of law in Poland is the Constitution of the Republic of Poland of April 2, 1997, which was approved in a national referendum.

12. Legislative power is exercised by a bicameral parliament. Parliament consists of the Sejm with 460 MPs and a senate with 100 senators. Both deputies and senators are elected by direct general and secret parliamentary elections for a four-year term of office from the date of the first session. The main tasks of the Sejm and Senate are to legislate by passing laws and ratifying international agreements.

13. The Sejm and Senate elect a speaker and deputy speakers from among their members, who form a presidium. The Speaker of the Sejm is the highest representative of the lower house of parliament, chairs sessions of the Sejm and represents it externally. The Sejm and Senate also appoint parliamentary committees, which are responsible for preparing bills and drafts in the area of legislation and control.

14. The President, Government, Senate, a group of fifteen deputies or a parliamentary committee or a group of 100,000 citizens are entitled to a legislative initiative. The acts of law passed by the Sejm are considered by the Senate, which has the right to propose amendments or reject the act. After the rejection, the act is returned to the Sejm where an absolute majority in the presence of at least 230 MPs can reject the Senate's objection. An act passed by the Sejm and Senate is then forwarded to the President, who can accept and sign it or veto and return it to the Sejm within twenty-one days for reconsideration or submit a motion to the Constitutional Tribunal to examine the compliance of the act with the Constitution. A presidential veto may be rejected by the Sejm with a three-fifths majority in the presence of at least 230 MPs.

15. The legal system in Poland is of a statutory law nature, based on statutes and ratified international agreements. Court judgments do not have legislative force.

16. The executive authorities in Poland are the President of the Republic of Poland and the council of ministers. The President is elected in general presidential elections for a five-year term of office. He may hold this office for a maximum of two terms. The President is the highest representative of the state in domestic and international relations. He is the head of the armed forces of the Republic of Poland. His powers include, but are not limited to signing statutes passed by the Sejm and Senate, ratifying international agreements, appointing judges and granting citizenship.

17. The council of ministers is a collegial body of the executive. It consists of the chairman of the council of ministers (prime minister), deputy prime ministers, ministers and chairmen of committees.

18. The bodies of the judiciary in Poland are the Supreme Court, the ordinary courts and the special courts. The latter include military and administrative courts. Together with the Tribunal of State and the Constitutional Tribunal, they form the independence of the judiciary.

19. Poland currently has eighty-five registered political parties. Poland has a minimal electoral threshold of 5% in elections to the Sejm, which means that, in practice, only the few largest groups have their representatives in the Sejm.

20. Poland is the sixth-largest economy in the European Union (in terms of GDP) and is still one of the fastest-growing economies in Europe.

IV. Population and Employment Statistics

21. Poland has a population of over 38,000,000. It is in sixth place in the European Union in terms of population.

22. The unemployment rate in October 2023 was 5%. The number of unemployed registered with labor offices is just over 770,000. In comparison, it is worth noting that the rate of unemployment was 20% in 2002 and 2003. The current rate of unemployment is the lowest it has been in thirty years.

23. The employment structure in the Polish economy differs slightly from the European norm. Over 8% of the population works in agriculture (the EU average is 5%). Industry, however, employs over 30% (the average for the European Union is 25%).

V. Enterprise, Corporation and Partnership Statistics

24. Limited liability companies are decidedly the most popular form of company in Poland, accounting for 450,000 of the total of almost 550,000 registered commercial companies and partnerships. General partnerships are next, accounting for just over 35,000, followed by around 30,000 limited partnerships, 12,000 joint-stock companies, around 4,000 mixed joint-stock and limited companies and the least popular professional partnerships, of which there are almost 2,500.[1]

25. Over 285,000 entities operate as civil partnerships (which—contrary to the name—is not an independent legal form).

26. Decidedly the most popular form of doing business in Poland is the simplest form, namely the registration of business activity by sole proprietors. There are over 2,500,000 such people in Poland. However, the vast majority of them are actually employed. Many people who actually work full-time are encouraged by employers or themselves to switch to self-employment because of the tax benefits and the reduction in the burden of social security contributions. Their obligations remain unchanged, they are still supervised by the current employer, but they formally provide services—from their business—to another entity under a personal service contract, a specific task contract or a cooperation agreement. Politicians from various parties have been announcing changes in this area for years and the forced transfer of people, whose activities have little to do with conducting business, understood as activities conducted at their own risk and to their own account, to full-time employment in the meaning of labor law. However, no such change has been introduced to date.

VI. Social and Cultural Values

27. Poland lies within an area of Latin civilization. A large proportion of the Polish public declares an attachment to traditional, conservative values, while the family is of key importance. However, there is also a large group of people advocating progressive values preached by leading liberal and leftist political parties.

28. Education in state schools and state universities is completely free. One of the oldest universities in Europe is located in Poland—the Jagiellonian University.

29. Poland has a rich cultural history, both in literature, theatre and in music. The most frequently mentioned Polish composers of classical music are Fryderyk Chopin, Karol Szymanowski and Krzysztof Penderecki. Andrzej Wajda and Roman Polański are mentioned among the filmmakers. Several Polish writers are winners of the Nobel Prize in literature. The best-recognized Polish writer today is Andrzej Sapkowski, whose books are among the top positions on the New York Times bestseller lists (largely due to the international success of The Witcher video game—published by a once small gaming start-up and now one of Poland's largest companies—CD Project, as well as the series on the Netflix portal of the same title).

1. Cf. data from A. Koch & J. Napierała, *Prawo spółek handlowych* [eng. *Commercial Companies Law*], 2019, p. 314.

30. Since the Second World War, which brought severe losses to art, most of that which was destroyed has been rebuilt and reconstructed, while a large proportion of looted monuments have been recovered.

31. Poland is also part of the global tourist market. Some Polish cities appear to have more foreigners than Poles in their centers in the summer.

VII. Privatization Efforts and Golden Shares

32. Profound ownership changes took place in Poland between 1945 and the end of the 1970s. The most extensive were conducted in 1945–1955. The whole of industry, trade, transport and banking were nationalized in those years. Property rights were severely restricted. Essentially, only the state was able to do business. Poles were largely deprived of the opportunity to run a business. The exceptions were only small-scale production, crafts/tailors, cobblers, etc., and—to a limited extent—farmers. However, the majority of production in agriculture was conducted within the framework of so-called state-owned farms organized on the basis of the principles of managing state property.

33. It was not until the economic collapse that took place in 1989 that stopped the trend of deepening the development of the socialist economy. The socialist authorities admitted the development of the private sector to a limited extent to counteract the effects of the huge economic crisis. In 1979–1989, namely before the transformations in 1989, national income generated by the public sector declined by 6.6%, while national income generated by companies and private farms increased by 26.2%.[2] Therefore, even at the end of the 1980s, before the turbulent political changes, there was a certain adjustment of the ownership structure in the generation of national income, through the slight decline in the state sector.

34. This adjustment, which involved the gradual departure from rigid socialist dogmas of a centrally planned economy, also applied to the way in which state enterprises operated. The departure from the centrally planned economy started at the beginning of the 1980s, towards a new model of enterprise, symbolized by the so-called three S—self-governance, self-reliance and self-financing.[3]

35. Self-reliance of state-owned enterprises enabled them to gain autonomy in decision-making with regard to their activities. According to this principle, state-owned enterprises were awarded the rank of separate business entities. This was about launching certain, albeit limited, market competition and operating on the basis of economic cost accounting, which was not the norm in earlier times.

---

2. Cf. statistical yearbook 1990, *Central Statistical Office*, Warsaw 1991, p. 120.
3. Cf. S. Szmitka, *Specyfika cech prywatyzacji polskiej gospodarki początkowego okresu reform* [eng. *Particular Traits of the Privatization of the Polish Economy in the Initial Phase of the Reforms*], p. 84.

36. Self-financing involved the introduction of the principle that the company was to obtain funds for investments by generating profits and gaining credibility with the bank providing loans.

37. However, self-governance involved granting extensive powers to the workers' council. The workers' council gained extensive participative rights in managing the enterprise. The high level of importance of employee participation arose from the fact that it guaranteed the legitimacy of the reformist intentions of the socialist authorities. As noted, giving employees the right to participate in company management was a poor substitute for democracy in times when free elections were not held in Poland.[4]

38. In 1989, the socialist authorities took up a dialogue with the solidarity opposition that was still operating illegally at the time. As a result, a round table was held, as were partially free parliamentary elections and the first noncommunist government was formed with Tadeusz Mazowiecki as the prime minister. Therefore, a significant political turnaround took place.

39. The political changes in Poland, which started in 1989, led to transformations in virtually all areas of life, from culture and sports to the legal system. The social changes, changes in the social structure and changes in people's awareness were taking place at a very fast pace. Economic changes were also a key element of the structural and political changes. One of the significant changes was the privatization of state assets that had been announced and implemented over successive decades. The legal grounds for the privatization of state property were provided by the Act on the Privatization of State-Owned Enterprises and the Management of Agricultural property of the State Treasury, the Act on National Investment Funds and their Privatization, and the Act on the Commercialization and Privatization of State-Owned Enterprises.

40. Several privatization paths were implemented in Poland. The largest enterprises were privatized through capital privatizations. They were initially transformed into companies in which the State Treasury was the sole shareholder, after which the stocks or shares of these companies were acquired by investors. These investors were both Polish and foreign investors. The latter had a definite advantage in the first decade of the transformations because of access to capital. Small and medium-sized enterprises and those that were in financial difficulty benefited from the liquidation path, namely direct privatization. In this path, state assets were sold, contributed to the companies or handed over for paid use.[5]

41. Agricultural land of state-owned farms was included in the State Treasury's so-called agricultural property resource.

---

4. Cf. S. Szmitka, *Specyfika cech prywatyzacji polskiej gospodarki początkowego okresu reform*, p. 85.
5. Cf. J. Kaliński, *Prywatyzacja w Polsce po 1989 r.* [eng. *Privatization in Poland after 1989*], p. 3.

42. Notwithstanding the above, in addition to the top-down privatization, bottom-up privatization was also developing rapidly with the participation of domestic and foreign capital.

43. A specially formed Ministry of Ownership Transformations managed privatizations from 1990. This topic has been the responsibility of the Ministry of the Treasury since 1996.

44. The Warsaw Stock Exchange was established in 1991. The first companies listed on the stock exchange were industrial and construction companies. Only a few companies were initially listed on the stock exchange in order to grow to around 400 companies over twenty years.

45. As reported in the literature, from 1990 to 2008, the total value of foreign capital invested in Poland in the form of direct foreign investments was almost EUR 115,000,000,000. Foreign capital demonstrated the greatest interest in the privatization of Polish companies from 1999 to 2001. At its peak, the share of foreign capital in privatization revenues was as high as 82%, to decline in 2004 to 9%.[6] Companies from Germany, the United States and France played the leading role in the privatization of Polish enterprises.

46. Intensive privatization lasting twenty years meant that only 363 state-owned enterprises operated in Poland in 2008, which was just 5% of the number at the beginning of the 1990s (Structural changes in groups of entities in the national economy in 2009, Central Statistical Office, Warsaw 2010, p. 30). After all, most of the remaining enterprises were struggling. It was quite widely accepted at that time that all state-owned enterprises should be privatized quickly.

47. The banking sector also underwent a full transformation. In the early 1990s, the nine largest regional branches were separated from the National Bank of Poland, as the state bank, the issuing bank and the bank of banks, which formed a network of state-owned banks of a universal nature. In 1995, these banks were transformed into joint-stock companies owned by the State Treasury and preparations for their privatization started. The first to be privatized and floated on the stock exchange were Wielkopolski Bank Kredytowy SA and Bank Przemysłowo Handlowy SA, as well as Bank Rozwoju Eksportu SA. After the changes in equity, the private sector's share of banking assets was over 80%. Simultaneously, foreign capital had a share of more than 70% of the banking sector's assets.[7]

48. The assessment of 1989–2000 is not unambiguous in Poland. Two opposing views should be mentioned.

---

6. Cf. J. Kaliński, *Prywatyzacja w Polsce po 1989 r.*, p. 5.
7. Cf. *Rozwój systemu finansowego w Polsce w 2008 r.*, red. P. Sobolewski & D. Tymoszko [eng. *Development of the Financial System in Poland in 2008*, eds P. Sobolewski & D. Tymoszko], National Bank of Poland, Warsaw 2009, p. 95.

49. According to the first of these, extensive privatization was a mistake. It meant giving away state assets for pittance and consolidation of the dominance of foreign capital in Poland for many decades. The reforms conducted did not take into account the needs of the employees of the privatized workplaces and the population. According to the proponents of this view, faith in the invisible hand of the market turned out to be a naivety. The increase in the country's national income did not translate into the public becoming more affluent. Reforms were conducted without protecting people against the effects of the systemic changes, as a result of which the social costs of the reforms were too high. The changes were accused of not taking into account both strong pro-employee trends in Polish society and the fact of having a very weak market infrastructure. While the equivalent privatization model based on the British experience, which was actually introduced in Poland, did not take into account Poland's specifics. Therefore, the proponents of this view accuse Polish privatization of having made a number of systemic errors, such as the lack of public acceptance of the reforms and reliance on privatization based on foreign capital.[8] According to one researcher, the liberal option, which actually had the real political power throughout the entire transformation period, applied the concept of creative destruction. It assumed that everything created between 1945 and 1989 should be destroyed and modern export-oriented sectors of the economy should be created in its place, which are fully competitive on world markets, thanks to foreign capital.[9]

50. Whenever they come to power, the proponents of this view consistently try to reverse the effects of the privatization, through the acquisition of previously privatized enterprises by state-owned companies. A good example of this is the banking sector. In the last ten years, the state has regained control of several banks, that had been previously privatized or which had been established from scratch as private entities. The views of the representatives of the current political authorities in Poland are similar to such views.

51. According to the second view, the reforms that were carried out had never been completed and privatization was not sufficiently deep and widespread. Many areas of Polish public life are still controlled by the state. Actual privatization has never taken place—despite being listed and private investors being admitted a minority share in some companies in areas from the broadly understood energy, mines, health care and public television. The economy has been insufficiently de-bureaucratized. The tax system has not been reformed sufficiently deeply.

52. This study is not a place for attempting to make a greater assessment of privatization. However, it should be clearly stated that the transformation privatization conducted in Poland was a reform of an incomparable scale. It was conducted in an impoverished society with a very weak market infrastructure. The

---

8. Cf. S. Szmitka, *Specyfika cech prywatyzacji polskiej gospodarki początkowego okresu reform*, p. 88.
9. Cf. A. Prusek, *Prywatyzacja polskiej gospodarki. Cele, programy i ocena ich rezultatów* [eng. *Privatization of the Polish Economy. Objectives, Programs and Assessment of Their Results*], Kraków 2005, pp. 15–16.

pressure to privatize also meant that actual mass reprivatization never actually took place in Poland, meaning the return by the state of what had been nationalized—taken by the state from private owners after 1945—in breach of the provisions of the law or even in accordance with socialist law. Several draft restitution bills have been prepared, but none of them has become an applicable act of law.

§2. The Historical Background of Corporations and Partnerships

53. Poland recovered its independence at the end of the First World War in 1918. At the time of recovery of independence, Poland had five different legal systems of its former partitioning states. The main task facing lawyers was to harmonize the regulations in force in the country and to create their own Polish, uniform legislation throughout the country. Regulations in all areas of law needed to be harmonized.

54. One of the important areas in which intensive unification work began was the area of commercial law. A commercial law section was established within the codification committee shortly after Poland regained independence. This section prepared specific bills in the area of commercial law, namely the Bill of Exchange Act, the Check Act and the Act on Joint Stock Companies. The work ended as late as 1934 when the first part of the Commercial Code came into effect.

55. The Commercial Code of 1934 encompassed two books. The first book contained provisions on merchants, including standards of company law, while the second book applied to commercial activities.

56. The Commercial Code of 1934 was based on the German Commercial Code of 1897. However, it also contains a large number of original solutions.

57. The Commercial Code was formally in force until 2001, but in fact, the vast majority of the provisions of the Commercial Code had been repealed as early as 1964. Only the provisions of the Commercial Code that applied to the general partnership, the limited liability company, the joint-stock company, the commercial register and official commercial representation remained in force.

58. The reasons for the actual repeal of the decided majority of the provisions of the Commercial Code in 1964 were complex. On the one hand, the key reason was doubtless the change in the economic and political system that took place in Poland in 1945, when Poland actually came under the control of the Soviet Union. As a result, a socialist system was imposed in Poland, with the primacy of state ownership over private ownership. The Prewar Commercial Code, which had been prepared in a different economic and political system, in which freedom of enterprise was one of the main principles of law, did not suit the new times. On the other hand, the Polish legal doctrine that had been developed in the 1950s and 1960s firmly supported the position of uniformity of civil law. It was acknowledged that the two-tier regulation of private law, which was divided into civil law and commercial law, is incompatible with the new socialist model of society. This was another reason for the repeal of the Commercial Code and the takeover of many of its provisions by the new civil legislation. Starting from 1964, Poland is therefore a country that was actually deprived of separate, comprehensive commercial codes.

59. It should also be clearly admitted that commercial law lost its significance after 1945. The so-called socialized trading, namely internal economic relations between the so-called socialized economy units, and therefore actually trading between state-owned enterprises controlled by the political authority became important. It was only in the 1980s that academic papers on classical business trading started to appear.

60. The discussion about the structure of Polish private law restarted in the 1990s, after the fall of socialist rule in Central and Eastern Europe. And the discussion then restarted on whether to remain with the principle of unity of civil law or whether to return to the Prewar principle of dualism of private law, with two separate codes—the Commercial Code and the Civil Code. The decision was ultimately made to leave the model which had been in force since 1964, namely the uniformity of civil law.

61. Consequently, a certain share of regulations on professional business trading is contained in the Civil Code in Poland to this day. An example would be the regulation regarding a special power of attorney, namely the official commercial representation of entrepreneurs. However, Poland also has a number of detailed regulations, which are separate from the Civil Code, regarding individual issues related to professional business trading. The key Act on this will be the Code of Commercial Companies and Partnerships (CCCP), which comprehensively regulates the method of establishing and functioning, as well as transforming and merging commercial companies, both partnerships and companies. In addition, a number of acts on specific areas of professional business trading, such as the insurance market, stock exchanges, financial institutions and so on are applicable under Polish legislation.

62. The key act of law regarding company law, the CCCP, was developed in the late 1990s. The draft commercial company law was also reviewed by a team of experts appointed by the *Stiftung für internationale rechtliche Zusammenarbeit*, the membership of which included Professors E. Heinecke, A. Baier, E. Pelzer and M. Lutter. The team acknowledged that the draft was fully in line with European Union law and was also recommended. The bill was assessed as the best among all the bills on company law from Central and Eastern Europe assessed so far by the foundation.[10]

10. Cf. S. Włodyka, (in:) S. Włodyka, *System prawa handlowego, tom drugi, prawo spółek handlowych* [eng. *System of Commercial Law, Volume 2, Commercial Company Law*], Warsaw 2012, p. 10.

63. Polish literature refers to two main reasons for passing a new comprehensive legal regulation of commercial company law in 2000.

64. First of all, it was rightly noted that the Commercial Code of 1934, which was only in force in its rudimentary form, did not suit modern, developed business practices. It was also rightly pointed out that the provisions of company law had essentially been irrelevant in Poland for almost fifty years, namely from 1945 to 1989. It had been essentially inadmissible for private individuals to conduct business. The state controlled the whole of commercial life. This is why the doctrine of the law and judicial decisions, which would actually adapt these Prewar provisions to the new challenges, had not developed in Poland.

65. Second, the need for the new regulation of commercial company law was dictated by the need to adapt Polish law to EU law, as a result of the perspective of Poland's forthcoming accession to the European Union.

66. The CCCP of 2000 was based on three fundamental principles. The first is the principle of the limited autonomy of commercial company law. The second is the principle of continuity and the third is compliance with European standards.

67. The principle of limited autonomy of commercial company law means that commercial company law falls under the broadly-understood civil law. It is a specialized part of the uniform civil law, not an independent branch of law.

68. In turn, the principle of continuity means that the grounds for the solutions of the CCCP were the solutions, concepts and terminology of the Commercial Code. The CCCP therefore refers to and creatively develops the solutions of the Commercial Code without trying to rebuild the regulations from scratch.

69. However, the principle of adapting to European standards means that Polish law was harmonized with the applicable provisions of European law with the best examples of solutions from the Member States of the European Union taken into account.

70. As can be seen from the above, Polish commercial legislation is an example of a monistic system of private law—a system of uniform civil law. Switzerland, Italy and the Netherlands also have such systems. The Polish system of private law differs from the Swiss and Italian models in that commercial company law was not encompassed by a uniform regulation of the Civil Code, but constitutes the subject of a separate normative act, namely the CCCP.[11] Therefore, in a certain sense, the Polish model falls between the classic model of the dualistic system of private law and the monistic system of private law, in which—in its classical model—the problems of commercial companies are regulated in the Civil Code.

---

11. Cf. S. Włodyka (in:) S. Włodyka, *System prawa handlowego, tom pierwszy, prawo handlowe: część ogólna* [eng. *System of Commercial Law, Volume 1, Commercial Law: General Section*], Warsaw 2009, pp. 10–11.

71. The nature of the system of regulation of private law is obviously also relevant to the legal nature of commercial law. In the dualistic system, commercial law is treated as a separate branch of law. In the monistic system, commercial law is understood purely as a section of civil law or, at most, a separate legal discipline.

§3. Definitions and Structure of Corporations and Partnerships

I. Different Forms of Corporations and Partnerships

A. General Partnership

72. The general partnership was regulated in Poland for the first time in the Commercial Code of 1934 and the provisions of that code were in force for over sixty years, until the end of 2000, when they were replaced by the comprehensive Act that is in force to this day, the CCCP.

73. A general partnership is a partnership which conducts a business under its own trade name and is not just another commercial company. In the Polish legal system, a general partnership is therefore the basic and simplest form of company constituting the starting point for other forms of company. In a general partnership, every partner is liable for the partnership's liabilities without limitation with all of their assets, jointly and severally with the remaining partners and the partnership. The liability of the partners is:

- Unlimited. This means that the partners are liable for the partnership's liabilities without any restrictions. Such liability is justified by the fact that the regulations on general partnerships do not provide for obligations regarding the contribution of a minimum level of capital, and therefore do not sufficiently protect the real value of the fund arising from contributions or the partnership's assets against activities that could potentially be detrimental to creditors.
- Joint and several. This means that every partner is responsible for the partnership's liabilities jointly and severally with the other partners and the partnership. This is passive solidarity. Therefore, the creditor may demand all or a part of the performance from all debtors jointly, from several of them or from each of them individually. The satisfaction of the creditor by any of the debtors releases the remaining debtors. The debtors are jointly and severally liable until the creditor is completely satisfied.
- Subsidiary. This means that the partnership's creditor may conduct enforcement against a partner's assets only if the enforcement of the partnership's assets proves unsuccessful. However, the creditor may bring an action before the enforcement of the assets is effective. Litigation against a partner in a partnership may end earlier, even before enforcement against the partnership is conducted. However, it is important that it is only when enforcement from the partnership's assets proves to be ineffective that it will be possible to conduct enforcement from the partner's assets. It is therefore possible to both sue the partner, together with the partnership, sue the partner separately from the partnership and obtain

an enforcement order against him that is subject to subsidiarity, as well as to sue a partner only after unsuccessful enforcement against the partnership or to sue only the partnership and obtain an enforcement title against it, and then obtain an enforcement clause to this title against a shareholder in the event of the unsuccessful enforcement against the partnership.[12]

- Unconditionally applicable. This means that the contractual provisions between the partners that do not comply with the principles of the liability of the partners do not incite an effect on third parties. They can be binding on partners, but they are ineffective externally.

74. Under Polish law, a general partnership is treated as a model partnership which realizes the personal nature of the partnership to the fullest possible extent. In a general partnership, the membership is permanent; each partner has the right to manage the partnership's affairs and to represent it. The name of the partnership must include the surname or trade name of at least one partner; each partner is responsible for the partnership's obligations without limitation with all of their assets, the partnership has no legal personality, the partner may work for or provide services to and make a contribution to the partnership. A partnership must have at least two partners.

75. Some but not all of the above elements may be modified by the partners themselves. For example, any changes in the principles of liability and an attempt to limit liability for the partnership's liabilities to some partners will not be effective in external relations.

76. A general partnership operates under its own name. The partnership's objective is to manage a business.

77. A general partnership has no legal personality, but it has legal identity and therefore may enter into contracts on its own behalf; it also has its own assets, which are separate from the assets of the partners. It may sue other parties and be sued.

B. Limited Partnership

78. The limited partnership was created over 800 years ago in medieval Italy. Businesses were established there, which were run by at least two participants, one of whom managed the enterprise externally, while the other only contributed money or goods. Meanwhile, the income was split among both partners. In Romanesque countries, this form of cooperation was defined as *commenda*. The German name—*Kommanditgeselschaft*—came from this definition and was then transferred into Polish (*spółka komandytowa*).[13]

12. Cf. judgment of the Constitutional Tribunal of Oct. 3, 2017, S K 31/15, decision of the Constitutional Tribunal, A 2017/62.
13. Cf. A. Koch & J. Napierała, *Prawo* ..., p. 287.

79. The limited partnership appeared in Polish law at the time that the Commercial Code was adopted, i.e., 1934; such companies operated for five years until the outbreak of the Second World War and for almost twenty years after the War. The limited partnership was restored to Polish law by restoring the Commercial Code to it in 1991, whereby the new regulation was essentially a copy of the Prewar regulations.

80. This regulation was in force until 2001 when a completely new Act on commercial companies was passed—the Code of Commercial Companies—which also included a regulation on a limited partnership.

81. The regulation on the limited partnership is rudimentary in Polish law and primarily applies to the regulation of the status of a partner whose liability for obligations is limited (limited partner). In terms of the legal status of a partner who is liable for the partnership's obligations with all his assets (general partner), the provisions on general partnerships apply accordingly. A characteristic feature of a limited partnership is precisely the presence of two types of partners—limited partners and a general partner. While the liability of the former is limited to a predetermined amount (limited amount), the liability of the general partner is unlimited.

C. Limited Joint-Stock Partnership

82. A limited joint-stock partnership in Polish law is structurally similar to a limited partnership. As in the last partnership, the limited joint-stock partnership also has a connection between an active investor and a passive investor. A limited joint-stock partnership is a hybrid company, combining the features of both partnerships and companies. It is emphasized in the Polish literature that it is also an interesting alternative to a joint-stock company. However, limited joint-stock partnerships constitute less than 1% of all registered commercial companies and partnerships.

83. The features of a limited joint-stock partnership that are specific to partnerships primarily include the existence of the category of partners who are liable for the company's liabilities with their personal assets (general partners) and the fact that it is precisely those partners who represent the company and handle its affairs. Likewise, the lack of legal personality, the obligation to include the name of at least one general partner in the partnership's name, as well as the treatment of the death and declaration of bankruptcy of the sole general partner as a reason for dissolving the partnership are also typical features of partnerships.

84. However, the features of a limited joint-stock partnership that are specific to companies include the existence of the category of equity shareholders—stockholders, the existence of a general meeting, the ability to appoint a supervisory board, and the existence of capital divided into stocks.

D. Professional Partnership

85. In contrast with many other forms of commercial companies, the history of a professional partnership is relatively short and can be traced very precisely. The first legislation regarding professional partnerships was adopted in Texas, United States, in response to numerous lawsuits against partners of law firms as a result of the crisis in the insurance market in the 1990s. The popularity among the Texas lawyers that the new legal form began to enjoy immediately encouraged subsequent states in the United States to enact similar laws. Just like Hollywood films, the professional partnership then became very popular and was included in the legislation of many countries, including Polish legislation. The CCCP introduced the professional partnership into Polish law.

86. The model of the professional partnership which applies in Poland is a kind of hybrid of the American model and the German model. This legal form in Polish law is addressed to a larger public than just lawyers, although it is the most popular in legal circles. According to the model adopted in Poland, the liability of individual partners for the partnership's liabilities related to an error committed by another partner or a person under his supervision is ruled out. All partners in a professional partnership have unlimited liability for all other liabilities in the same way as partners in a general partnership.

E. Limited Liability Company

87. A limited company is decidedly the most popular form of company in Poland. The popularity of this legal form is related to the implementation of two assumptions. The first of these assumptions is the separation of the company's assets from the assets of the shareholders and the exclusion of the personal liability of the shareholders for the company's liabilities. The second is the relatively uncomplicated procedure of establishing and operating a company. In terms of the latter element, it should be pointed out, among others, that, a limited liability company has decidedly fewer cases—compared to a joint-stock company—of the need for a notary public to record respective activities undertaken at the company. The services of statutory auditors also need to be used to a minor extent.

88. The formal requirements that are envisaged for joint-stock companies are clearly visible when comparing a limited company with a joint-stock company. The relatively large amount of freedom of the shareholders of limited liability companies in shaping their internal model—the structure and method of operation—is even invisible.

89. A limited liability company is a company. It has all the features of companies in many other countries. Its equity nature is manifested in the fact that it has a legal personality, the assets of the shareholders are completely separated from the company's assets, the shareholders are not liable for the company's liabilities, while the company's assets cannot constitute a subject of enforcement that would satisfy a shareholder's personal creditor.

90. Despite the name, the liability of the company itself to its creditors obviously does not have any restrictions. The company itself is liable for its liabilities without restrictions. Its shareholders are not liable for the company's liabilities.

91. However, a limited liability company has certain personal elements such as those found in partnerships.

92. The shareholders have the right to exercise personal control over the company's activities and operations. In a joint-stock company, the shareholders do not have this right, while their only actual indirect controlling right is the right to choose the members of the supervisory board, which then controls the management board's activities. In a limited liability company, the shareholders cannot be deprived of the ability to review the ledgers and documents or to obtain information on the company's state of affairs and assets. Only in larger companies, i.e., those which have more than twenty-five shareholders and the share capital is over PLN 500,000 is it obligatory to appoint a supervisory board or an audit committee (The amounts in this monograph are quoted in PLN. The exchange rate is available on the Polish central bank's website) (Narodowy Bank Polski).

93. The personal element in the structure of a limited liability company is also the ability of a court to exclude a shareholder and dissolve the company.[14]

94. The articles of association can also rule out or limit the right of heirs of a deceased shareholder to join the company.

95. The last element mentioned in the Polish legal doctrine as a personal element in a limited liability company is the admissibility of the general meeting of shareholders to issue binding recommendations to the management board on matters related to the management of the company's affairs.[15] This is important because a joint-stock company's general meeting is prohibited from issuing binding instructions to the management board.

96. A limited liability company may be established for any legally permissible purpose unless otherwise arises from the provisions governing specific activities which the company intends to conduct. Therefore, a limited liability company does not need to be established for a business objective. It is admissible to establish a limited company for non-profit purposes. It is also permissible to establish a limited liability company for it to earn an income from its participation in other entities, namely as a holding company.

---

14. Articles 266 and 271 CCCP.
15. Cf. A. Koch & J. Napierała, *Prawo* … , p. 335.

97. Polish regulations regarding a limited liability company are largely influenced by German legal thought.

F. Joint-Stock Company

98. A joint-stock company is a classic form of a company used to conduct larger-scale business. The structure of a joint-stock company makes it relatively easy to raise capital for development from a wide range of investors. The management of a joint-stock company is in the hands of specialized managers, while the owners (the general meeting) do not have the right to issue binding instructions on the management of the company's affairs to the management board (although it should be pointed out that the latter issue is disputable in the Polish legal doctrine and work is currently underway to relax this prohibition).

99. Stockholders are not responsible for the company's liabilities. A stockholder actually only risks the contribution he made to the company.

100. Stockholders also have the right to dispose of the company's shares at any time. The unlimited transferability of equity rights reduces the cost of raising capital by joint-stock companies.

101. The significance of the capital market is much smaller in the Polish economy than in developed Western markets. The share of capital inflows obtained by public joint-stock companies on the capital market in relation to the total gross outlay on fixed assets of enterprises is negligible. The stock exchange does not play a major role in the valuation and control of Polish enterprises. Many key enterprises are managed in the form of limited liability companies. Many public companies, which are run in the form of joint-stock companies, are controlled by the State Treasury, while the method of managing them is highly unclear. Anomalies arise, involving very low valuations of large listed companies, sometimes at a level of only two or three times annual earnings, which, even so, are not treated as attractive investment opportunities. This arises from the fact that these companies, being controlled by the State Treasury, are under the actual influence of politicians, while the investment decisions they make are often not based on a simple profit and loss account, but also take into account political factors such as the need to subsidize unprofitable sectors of the Polish economy (such as the coal mines).

102. The very structure of a joint-stock company is similar to that of joint-stock companies in many developed Western legislations. A joint-stock company is a classic company, in which management is separated from ownership. A joint-stock company is a highly formalized legal form. Many activities require the presence of a notary public. The role of statutory auditors is also important.

II. Distinction Between Structures and Consequences

103. The differences between Polish and American law with regard to company law are fundamental and apply to such a basic issue as distinguishing between different forms of company. A U.S. company cannot be unambiguously qualified and its nature cannot be determined purely by its name. This is because the demarcation between civil partnerships and commercial companies under U.S. law is not as clear-cut as under Polish law. Under Polish law, the mere name of the company is already an absolutely clear signal indicating the legal nature of the company and, in particular, whether it will have legal personality.

104. The differences between the individual legal forms of company in Poland are significant and visible at first glance. A limited liability company is almost always the entity of first choice for anyone intending to start up a business.

105. A general, professional, limited partnership and a limited joint-stock partnership are chosen much less frequently.

106. A joint-stock company is only chosen by entities that will be thinking of flotation on the stock exchange in the near future or the investment plans of the founders assume the need to raise capital from a large group of investors. After all, the Polish lawmakers have created a model of a so-called simple joint-stock company (Prosta spółka akcyjna (PSA)) for this last group. The requirements regarding the establishment and operation of such entities are much softer than the requirements of a classic joint-stock company.

107. However, on the sideline, it should be pointed out that, contrary to the name, the model of a PSA is not at all simple from the legal point of view. On the contrary, it is one of the most complex legal forms in Polish law. This arises from the fact that the regulations on the PSA are included in the CCCP. The PSA regulations are a modification of the existing regulations on joint-stock companies. Unlike in some other countries, Poland has not passed a separate law on simple joint-stock companies. However, the difficulties for lawyers dealing with this legal form should not create any difficulties in its practical operation. Even so, it was noted in the legal doctrine that this company is so flexible that it gives rise to concerns about the security of creditors—persons who enter into contractual relations with such entities.

108. Until the amendment of the CCCP introducing the PSA, the distinction between a big corporation and a closely held corporation did not pose any difficulties. The legal structure of a limited liability company and a joint-stock company are very different. The process of establishment is different, different rules govern the management of the company, and supervision issues are regulated differently. People starting a business or planning to set up another company usually have no problems choosing between one legal form and another. This choice was somehow automatic and depended on the level of the planned activity and the method of raising capital. Only the introduction into Polish law of the PSA constitutes a blemish on this clear distinction between a limited liability company and a joint-stock company. The PSA is structurally a joint-stock company, but it simultaneously offers an extensive amount of freedom and flexibility—in the absence of any capital requirements—to future shareholders. The choice between a limited liability company and a normal joint-stock company will no longer be so obvious. A PSA is still too new for any binding conclusions to be formulated. However, it should be pointed out that the Polish legal doctrine has essentially almost unanimously criticized both the mere fact that the legal structure of a PSA was introduced into Polish law and the way it was conducted (namely through modifications to the existing regulations on the joint-stock company instead of passing a separate act on the PSA).

109. The consequences of choosing a specific legal form by the founders are mitigated by the possibility of transforming the legal form of the company, which was introduced by the CCCP, without losing its legal existence. Therefore, for instance, there is no obstacle to transforming a limited liability company into a joint-stock company in a situation where the shareholders intend to conduct a flotation on the stock exchange.

110. A civil partnership also plays an important role in Polish law. This is despite the highly visible dislike by the legal world and the legal doctrine of this form of business activity. A civil partnership is only an agreement between two or more people on conducting business together. A civil partnership has no assets of its own, no legal personality and no legal identity; it cannot sue or be sued and does not have its own name. Despite this, it is highly popular in Poland. Civil partnerships manage large-scale enterprises in Poland and the partners try to give a civil partnership with quasi-authorities such as a management board, their own names, etc. The popularity of a civil partnership arises from the simplicity of both the establishment and the functioning in trading, with a low level of awareness of the risks related to running a business in this form.

III. Commercial and Civil Corporations and Partnerships

111. As briefly mentioned above, under Polish law, business activity may also be conducted in the form of civil partnerships. The matter of a civil partnership is not treated as a part of commercial law but under specific provisions of civil law. The practical effect of this division is that civil partnerships are not discussed in textbooks on commercial law. A civil partnership is an agreement regulated by the Polish Civil Code (PCC) in the provisions of Articles 860–875. The conclusion of a civil partnership agreement creates a contractual civil law relationship between its parties, on the basis of which the partners undertake to pursue a common economic goal by acting in a defined way, in particular by making contributions.[16]

16. Cf. A. Kidyba, *Prawo handlowe* [eng. *Commercial Law*], Warsaw 2019 and K. Pietrzykowski (in:) K. Pietrzykowski editorial office, *Kodeks Cywilny* [eng. *Civil Code*], Volume 2, p. 485.

112. The structure of a civil partnership is an obligation that is similar to obligations incurred under other contracts regulated by the PCC, such as a sales contract or a lease contract. However, the difference is that, by entering into this agreement, a special bond is created between the partners. Consequently, the actions taken by one partner affect both the other partners and third parties.[17]

113. Up to the early 2000s, the partnership itself was treated as a separate entrepreneur. The entry into force of the new Act at the beginning of 2001—on the National Court Register and the business activity—meant that, instead of treating a civil partnership as a separate entrepreneur, individual people who entered into a civil partnership agreement were treated as separate entrepreneurs. To this day, entrepreneurs themselves are partners in a civil partnership in the business activities which they perform.

114. In principle, a civil partnership operates with an unchanged membership. A partner may only join the partnership through a change in the partnership agreement. It is not possible to transfer shares in a civil partnership to a third party although, in this respect, the position of the Polish legal doctrine and case law is not uniform (in contrast, among others, the resolution of the Supreme Court of November 21, 1995, III CZP 160/95, OSNC 1996, No. 3, item 33).

115. The conclusion of a civil partnership agreement results in joint ownership between the partners, encompassing both contributions made to the partnership and all components acquired in the course of the civil partnership's activities. Therefore, the property that is created is the property of all partners, not of the partnership. Therefore, it is inadmissible to use the notion of the partnership's assets.

116. Additionally, the partnership has no legal identity and no legal personality. All partners are always parties to the legal transactions.

117. Every partner is entitled to handle the matters of the civil partnership. This right of the partner can only be taken away with his consent or by a court for valid reasons. The partners may also regulate the principles of handling matters in the partnership agreement. If they fail to do so, the statutory principles will apply. According to the statutory principles, each partner may handle affairs that do not exceed the scope of the partnership's ordinary activities without a prior resolution of the partners.[18] If the activities are activities that exceed the scope of the partnership's ordinary activities, all partners need to pass a resolution. If the act is of the nature of an act of ordinary management, but if even one of the partners objects to it being conducted before it is completed, a resolution of all partners is required.[19]

---

17. Cf. M. Litwińska, *Spółka cywilna w świetle nowych regulacji prawnych* [eng. *Civil Partnership*], PPH2001, No. 7, p. 13.
18. Article 865 §2 PCC.
19. Article 865 §2 PCC.

And finally, if an act is of an extraordinary nature, which, if not conducted, would expose the partnership to irreparable damage, each partner is able to perform such an act without a prior resolution.[20]

118. The differentiation between acts of ordinary management and extraordinary activities is explained in the Polish legal doctrine as follows. Acts of ordinary management are those acts which ensure that it is properly conducted in the normal course of the partnership's business.[21]

119. The principles presented above regarding handling the partnership's affairs also apply to representation in a civil partnership. Therefore, a partner has the right to represent a civil partnership if it applies to activities that do not exceed the scope of ordinary activities and if he is performing urgent activities, the omission of which could expose the partnership to irreparable damage. However, in the case of acts exceeding the scope of ordinary activities and acts that are indeed part of the partnership's normal activities, but with respect to which one of the partners has raised an objection, a resolution of the partners is required before taking such action (e.g., the conclusion of an agreement). A partner who performs legal acts while representing a civil partnership acts as its statutory representative.[22]

120. Each partner in a civil partnership is jointly and severally liable for the liabilities of the partners arising in connection with the civil partnership. Each partner in a civil partnership is therefore liable for the whole of the debt, while the fulfillment of a performance releases the other partners. Therefore, unlike in the case of commercial law companies, the liability of partners in a civil partnership is a primary responsibility and not a subsidiarity. The creditor will be able to reach for the personal assets of the partners even before attempting to enforce payment from the assets of the civil partnership (in fact from the assets of the partners built as part of the business of the civil partnership).

121. A civil partnership may be transformed into a general partnership.[23] The transformation requires the notification of the registry court by all partners. A civil partnership may also be transformed into another commercial company.

IV. Non-profit Associations and Other Corporate Legal Persons

122. Polish law provides for a whole range of *non-profit* and *not-for-profit* legal forms of organization. A common feature of these entities is that their objective is not to make a profit. Even if organizations of this type earn an income from doing

20. Article 865 §3 PCC.
21. Cf. A. Kidyba, *Prawo* ..., p. 251.
22. Cf. A. Kidyba, *Prawo* ..., p. 252.
23. Article 26 §4 CCCP.

business, it is only incidental to the primary objective, which differs from making a profit.

123. The legal nature of non-profit organizations varies greatly. The list of such entities includes not only associations and foundations but also political parties, Independent Public Healthcare Institutions, sports associations, the social professional organization of farmers, organizations, crafts and chambers of commerce.

124. The most important are, no doubt, foundations and associations.

125. The activities of foundations and the procedure of establishing a foundation in Polish law are regulated by relatively stringent legislation, especially compared to some Western jurisdictions. In particular, the foundation's ability to do business is significantly limited. A foundation's business should only be an accessory to the core activity which is not doing business. The core activity, namely the activity which is targeted at the objective for which the foundation was established, must be defined as generally as possible. Therefore, for example, foundations that have the intention of achieving a specific objective, not even economic, but related to a specific person or family, are not admissible.

126. A foundation can only start doing business on its own after satisfying several conditions.

127. First, the foundation's business activities and principles should be announced in the foundation's statutes.

128. Second, the activity will only be conducted to the extent to which it serves the foundation's statutory objectives.

129. Third, at least PLN 1,000 will be allocated to business activities.

130. Fourth, the foundation will be entered into the register of entrepreneurs of the National Court Register.

131. In turn, associations can be established for any legally permissible purpose. Over 97,000 associations are registered in Poland. Associations may also do business, but also after meeting certain conditions. The key conditions are the need to allocate the income from the association's business activities exclusively to the achievement of the association's statutory objectives and the prohibition to allocate the income from the association's business activities to distribution among the members of the association.

§4. Sources and Hierarchy of the Law on Corporations and Partnerships

I. International Sources

132. European company law, which contains a set of primary and secondary standards of European Union law for the functioning of the internal market, constitutes the matter of European law. The key rule of legal norms regarding this matter is the ability to guarantee the company the ability to exercise freedom of establishment in the meaning of Article 49 of the European Union Treaty. More details on European company law—regulations and directives, including the regulation on the European company and the regulation on the European Economic Interest Grouping—are contained in the study on European company law.

II. National Sources

A. *Legislation*

133. The main source of national company law is the CCCP of September 15, 2000, which entered into force on January 1, 2001, and repealed the Commercial Code of June 1934, leaving only those provisions of the Commercial Code that applied to the name of commercial companies and commercial representation in force. The latter provisions were subsequently repealed in 2003 after they were reregulated and introduced into the currently applicable Civil Code.

134. Work on the modernization of commercial company law itself has been ongoing since the mid-1990s. The assumptions to the draft CCCP were prepared by the commercial companies' team appointed in 1996. The team included Prof. Stanisław Sołtysiński, Prof. Andrzej Szajkowski and Prof. Janusz Szwaja, who was subsequently replaced by Prof. Andrzej Szumański. The draft CCCP was the subject of numerous discussions and consultations, including at a national meeting of commercial law departments of Polish universities in Szklarska Poręba in 1999, in which the author of this study had the opportunity to participate.

135. An additional source of law for commercial law companies will also be the PCC. The Civil Code exhaustively regulates issues related to the names of commercial companies and commercial representation, which constitutes a special power of attorney.

136. Many other laws regulating either individual issues related to running a business or issues related to specific types of business will also constitute sources of commercial law. All the provisions that apply to the operation of companies in which the State Treasury or local government units hold a stake, such as the Act on commercialization and certain employee rights of August 30, 1996, as well as the Act on the principles of setting salaries for people managing certain companies of June 9, 2016, which specifies the rules for setting the salaries of members of the management board and the supervisory board in companies in which the State Treasury or local government units have an equity stake, can also be mentioned as a separate group of regulations.

137. The provisions regarding the introduction of the National Court Register are also important.

138. The sources of law also include customs and good practices, to which certain provisions of the CCCP and the Civil Code refer.

B. Bylaws or Articles

139. The articles of association are of key importance and constitute an internal bylaw of that entity. The articles of association are used for the shareholders or stockholders to undertake to pursue a common goal by making contributions and—if the articles or bylaws so provide—by cooperating in a specific manner.[24]

140. The articles of association are signed by the shareholders. The company itself is not a party to the articles of association, the content of the articles of association defines the legal relations of the commercial company.

C. Relationship Between Bylaws or Articles and Legislation

141. The relationship between national legislation and the founding agreement is a relationship of subordination. The regulations arising from the founding agreement must not be in conflict with the statutory provisions. In many situations, however, the CCCP allows the shareholders to regulate specific issues in the articles of association differently than proposed by the lawmakers. This then applies to the so-called semi-dispositive provisions of the CCCP.

III. Hierarchy of the Law on Corporations and Partnerships

142. Immediately after the primary law of the European Union, the highest source of law in Poland is the Constitution of the Republic of Poland.

143. In the hierarchy of sources of law, the statutes come immediately after the Constitution. The key statute regarding commercial company law is the CCCP which was passed in 2000. The CCCP regulates key issues regarding the establishment and operation of all six commercial companies, together with their transformation, as well as mergers and divisions.

24. Article 3 of CCCP.

144. Regardless of the regulation of the matter regarding commercial companies in a separate Act, namely the CCCP, the Polish legal doctrine takes the position of the so-called unity of civil law. This means that the general provisions of the Civil Code should be applied to matters not covered by the CCCP. The principle is used to apply the provisions of the Civil Code directly and therefore without any modifications. For example, the provisions regarding the name of a commercial company and commercial representation are applied directly. Only if required by the nature of the commercial company's legal relations will the provisions of the Civil Code be applied accordingly (second sentence of Article 2 of the CCCP). Applying it accordingly means the need to make appropriate modifications to the wording of the provision of the Civil Code or the withdrawal from the application of the provisions of the Civil Code.

145. However, if certain issues are exhaustively regulated in the CCCP, the provisions of the Civil Code do not apply. Therefore, it would be inadmissible to establish a commercial company other than one of those listed in the CCCP.

§5. International Private Law (Conflict of Laws Rules)

146. Polish private international law (PIL) of February 4, 2011, contains a relatively broad regulation on the conflict-of-law problems of commercial law companies.[25]

147. A legal person is subject to the law of the country in which it is established.[26] However, if the law specified in accordance with the said doctrine provides for the jurisdiction of the country on the basis of which the legal person was established, the law of the latter country shall be applicable. However, PIL does not explicitly regulate the notion of the company's seat. The Polish doctrine on PIL and commercial law advocates understanding the seat as the registered office, in isolation of the actual seat of the management body.

148. All key issues regarding the functioning of a commercial company are subject to the law specified in accordance with the rules described in the foregoing paragraph. These are the establishment, merger, division, transformation or dissolution of a legal person, the legal nature of that legal person, the name and form of that legal person, the principles of operation, appointment and dismissal of members of the governing bodies and their powers, company representation, the acquisition of the status of shareholder and membership, the effects of a breach of the provisions of the generally applicable law and the statutory regulations by people representing the legal person, as well as the liability of the shareholders and members of the governing bodies for the company's obligations.[27]

---

25. Article 17.
26. Article 17, para. 1 PIL.
27. Article 17, para. 3 PIL.

149. The issue of selecting the law that is applicable to agreements before the establishment of the commercial company may be problematic. Most of the Polish legal doctrine is of the opinion that preliminary agreements to other contracts, which prepare agreements forming companies, should be governed by the law that applies to obligations.[28] In turn, the law of the registered office of the company should be applied to commercial companies at the stage of organization, such as limited liability companies and joint-stock companies which were established in the form of a notarial deed and have internal organizations or assets.[29]

150. This law, which is applicable to the company's statutes also specifies the material and legal conditions for its establishment, such as, for example, the number of people required to establish a company, the openness of the establishment of a single-person company, the admissibility of establishing a single-person company by another single-person company, etc.

151. The law that is applicable to the company's articles of association is also applicable to the assessment of the extent of the shareholders' liability for the company's debts. Likewise, issues regarding piercing the corporate veil will be assessed in accordance with the same law.

152. The articles of association of companies also apply to organizational units to which the law confers legal capacity. Under Polish law, these will be all partnerships, namely the general partnership, the limited partnership, the limited joint-stock partnership and the professional partnership.

153. As mentioned above, the articles of association of a legal person cover all matters related to its establishment and dissolution. Therefore, the law of the place of the company's registered office will cover all issues related to the individual stages of establishing the company, e.g., conclusion of organizational agreements, acquisition of shares, registration of the company, etc.

154. The articles of association also cover all matters related to the organization of the company, in particular the structure of the governing bodies and the powers of those bodies.[30] Local law of the place of the company's registered office is also applicable to the management of the company's affairs and the representation of the company by the shareholders. It arises from the above that attempts sometimes made in Poland to create a monistic management and supervisory body combining the functions of the management board and the supervisory board in Polish companies, i.e., a limited liability company or joint-stock company, are inadmissible. A governing body of this type can only function in a European company.

28. Article 28 PIL and consequently, the Rome I Regulation.
29. Cf. A. Koch & J. Napierała, *Prawo* ..., p. 732.
30. Article 17, para. 3, item 5 PIL.

§6. The Labor Law Connection: Co-determination and Corporate Structure

155. The regulations on this are relatively limited under Polish law. Among other things, the Act on commercialization and certain rights of employees of August 30, 1996, regulates the issues regarding the membership of supervisory boards of companies arising as a result of commercialization.[31]

156. In Poland, employees' participation in a company's governing bodies concerns companies created in the course of commercialization and privatization of state enterprises[32] and in the course of commercialization of public utilities.[33]

157. The Act on commercialization and privatization vests in the employees of a company created in the course of commercialization of a state enterprise the right to elect certain supervisory board members and (only in companies with an average annual complement of more than 500) also the right to elect one management board member. This means that the employees have a say in supervising and sometimes also in managing such companies—as both the supervisory board members and the management board member are granted access to all the information pertaining to the enterprise.[34]

158. Pursuant to Article 11 paragraphs 1–3 of the above Act, a joint-stock company created in the course of commercialization has a supervisory board. The number of the supervisory board members is set in the company's articles of association, it being understood that the first supervisory board comprises five members, including two employees' representatives. In companies created by way of transforming agricultural and food industry enterprises, farmers or fishers and employees are entitled to one representative each in the supervisory board.

159. Only in limited liability companies created in the course of commercialization is it possible not to appoint the supervisory board.

160. The manner of electing the supervisory board members by employees or by employees and farmers or fishers is set forth in the company's articles of association or in the bylaws enacted as provided for in the articles of association. Supervisory board members representing employees or employees and farmers or fishers are elected by direct, secret and general vote. Employees' representatives to the first supervisory board are elected by the general meeting of employees (delegates).

---

31. Articles 11–18 of that Act.
32. Articles 12–16 of the Act on commercialization and certain rights of employees of Aug. 30, 1996 (i.e., O.J.2023.343).
33. Article 18 of the Act on public utilities management of Dec. 20, 1996 (i.e., O.J.2021.679).
34. Cf. M. Smusz-Kulesza, *Przedstawiciele w organach spółek powstałych w wyniku prywatyzacji i komercjalizacji przedsiębiorstw państwowych* [w:] *Zbiorowe prawo pracowników do informacji*, 2012 [eng. *Representatives in Governing Bodies of Companies Created Through Privatization and Commercialization of State Enterprises* [in:] *Employees' Collective Right to Information*, 2012].

161. Failure to elect employees, farmers or fishers' representatives to the first supervisory board does not preclude entering the company in the register of entrepreneurs or adopting valid resolutions by the supervisory board.

162. Upon written request of at least 15% of the general complement, a vote to recall an employees' representative from the supervisory board may be held.

163. Pursuant to Article 14 paragraphs 1 and 2 of the Act on commercialization, as of the State Treasury ceasing to be the sole shareholder of the company created in the course of commercialization, the provisions of the articles of association pertaining to appointing and recalling the supervisory board members may be amended. Employees retain the right to elect two members of a supervisory board comprising seven to ten members and four members of that comprising eleven or more members. In companies created by way of transforming agricultural and food industry enterprises, farmers or fishers retain the right to elect one or two supervisory board members.

164. The vote results are binding on the general meeting. Thus, the seats intended for employees' representatives may not be taken by nonemployee-elected individuals.

165. Apart from employee representatives serving on the supervisory board of a commercialized state enterprise, the staff complement also has the right to elect their representative to the management board of the newly incorporated company, provided that the average annual complement at such company is more than 500. The rules and manner of electing and recalling the management board member by employees are set forth in the articles of association. The vote results are binding on the body appointing the management board.

166. Employees are also legally entitled to appoint approximately one-third of the supervisory board in a single-person limited liability company created through transforming a public utility. Employees are merely entitled to elect members of such boards, which does not mean that they must exercise this right.

167. Company employees elect, respectively: (1) Two members of a supervisory board comprising up to six members; (2) Three members of a supervisory board comprising seven to ten members; (3) Four members of a supervisory board comprising eleven or more members. Due to the fact that employees are entitled, not obliged, to elect supervisory board members, companies' articles of association or founding deeds must provide for such number of supervisory board members, so that failure to elect employee representatives to the board does not conflict with the requirement as to its minimum composition stipulated in the Code of Commercial Companies.[35]

---

35. Cf. C. Banasiński & K. M. Jaroszyński, *Komentarz do art. 18* [w:] C. Banasiński & K. M Jaroszyński, *Ustawa o gospodarce komunalnej Komentarz*, Warszawa 2017 [eng. C. Banasiński &

168. Employees' representatives in supervisory boards are elected by direct, secret and general vote. The vote results are binding on the general meeting.

169. The applicable provision[36] particularly safeguards the employment of company staff serving on the supervisory board. These safeguards essentially prohibit terminating supervisory board members during the supervisory board's term of office and for one year thereafter. The exception in this regard is the possibility to terminate in the cases listed in Article 52 of the Labour Code (i.e., with the employee being at fault for gross dereliction of duty). During the supervisory board's term of office and for one year thereafter, the company also may not downgrade the employee's employment or salary terms.

170. The provisions of the abovementioned acts prevail over Article 385 §3 and §5–9 of the Code of Commercial Companies and they waive group election (some of the shareholders elect one supervisory board member and do not participate in the election of the others) as to the seats taken pursuant to these provisions. Consequently, in companies subject to the abovementioned acts, group election may only concern such part of the board which is not appointed by employees. This conclusion is essential to determining the number of shares necessary to have a group able to elect a board member. Employee-elected supervisory board members reduce the number of seats to be taken by way of group election, thus raising the threshold of the number of shares legitimizing the election of a supervisory board member pursuant to Article 385 §5. Therefore, they render it difficult for the minority to elect a nominee. There is a natural propensity that institutionalized tools protecting the stakeholders' (here: the employees') interests inevitably weaken the shareholders' position, particularly that of the minority shareholders.[37]

171. Apart from state-owned companies and those created through transforming public utilities, employee participation in managing or supervising private companies is virtually nonexistent.

K. M. Jaroszyński, *Commentary to Article 18* [in:] C. Banasiński & K. M Jaroszyński, *Act on Public Utilities Management: Commentary*], Warsaw 2017.

36. Article 18, para. 6.

37. Cf. A Opalski, *Niektóre problemy wyboru grupowego członków rady nadzorczej* [eng. *A Opalski, Certain Problems with Group Elections of Supervisory Board Members*], PPH2015, No. 2, p. 40.

Part I. Corporations/Companies

Chapter 1. Big Corporation: Public Corporation—Share Company

§1. Characteristics

172. The number of joint-stock companies in Poland does not reflect their actual role. Poland has several dozen times more limited liability companies than joint-stock companies. However, the joint-stock company is chosen by the largest entities of key importance to the Polish economy. All public companies have the legal form of joint-stock companies.

173. A joint-stock company is the most developed form of commercial company under Polish law. The typical features of a joint-stock company include the complete separation of ownership functions in a company from its day-to-day management; limiting the liability of shareholders for the company's liabilities and the fully free transferability of the company's shares.

174. The shareholders do not have to be—they are usually not—involved in the day-to-day management of the company. The literature mentions that this enables the diversification of investment risk by shareholders because they can direct investment capital to many companies. In this way, they minimize risk in the event of the bankruptcy of one of these companies.

175. The shareholders are not liable for a joint-stock company's liabilities. In the case of the bankruptcy of the company, the shareholders only lose the capital invested in the shares.

176. The shares are fully freely traded. On the one hand, this reduces the costs of raising capital by the company, on the other hand, it allows investors to make quick decisions and implement them within their investment plans.

177. In principle, the shareholders may also leave the investment at any time, as long as someone is willing to purchase the shares.

178. The Polish literature indicates that Polish joint-stock companies operate in a closed corporate governance system. A closed corporate governance system means the concentration of shares in the hands of strategic investors. The dominant owner can therefore control the activities of the company's managers. Such capital market mechanisms as hostile takeovers are of limited significance.

§2. Formation

I. Formal Requirements (E.g., Notarial Record) and Minimum Content of Articles

179. A joint-stock company may be established in various ways. The basic way of establishing a joint-stock company is its formation. However, it is also possible to transform an existing company operating within a different legal form into a joint-stock company. It is also possible to merge or divide an existing company.

180. A joint-stock company's articles of association must be prepared in the form of a notarial deed.

181. The company's founders do not have to be the company's shareholders, although, in practice, the founders will be its shareholders.

182. A joint-stock company's articles of association should specify:[38]

- the company's name and registered address;
- the objects of the company;
- the term of the company if it is defined;
- the amount of share capital and the amount paid up before registration to cover the share capital;
- the nominal value of the shares and number indicating whether the shares are registered or bearer shares;
- the number of shares of particular types and their rights if shares of various types are to be introduced;
- surnames and forenames or trade names of the founders;
- the number of members of the management board and supervisory board or at least the minimum or maximum number of members of these bodies, as well as the entity authorized to specify the membership of the management board or the supervisory board;
- the place of announcements, if the company intends to make an announcement in a place other than the official journal, Monitor Sądowy i Gospodarczy (in which all announcements must be published);
- the number and types of titles to participation in the profit or in division of the company's assets and their related rights;
- all obligations to provide services to the company related to the shares, except the obligation to pay the receivables for the share;
- the conditions and method of redemption of the shares; restrictions on the transferability of the shares;

38. Article 304 §1–2 CCCP.

- personal rights awarded to the shareholders;
- at least an approximate level of all costs incurred or charged to the company in connection with its establishment.

183. The last six elements specified above should be included in the articles of association; otherwise, they will not be effective with respect to the company.

184. The founders may also include provisions in the articles of association regarding essentially all other matters unless a specific prohibition arises from the law.

185. The establishment of a joint-stock company requires the formation of the company, including the signature of the articles of association by the founders, contributions by the shareholders to cover the share capital, the appointment of the management board and the supervisory board, and—as the last step—the entry into the register of entrepreneurs.[39]

II. Notification, Registration, Incorporation and Publicity

186. A joint-stock company is only established after the entry is made in the register of entrepreneurs. The entry in the register is therefore constitutive. The register of entrepreneurs is publicly available and the basic data contained therein is public.

187. The establishment of a company is understood in Polish law as the conclusion of the founding agreement or the founding deed and the acquisition of all the shares—or the minimum number of shares in the case of an invitation in the articles of association specifying the minimum amount of share capital.

III. Contracts Made on Behalf of a Corporation/Company in Formation

188. A so-called joint-stock company in formation is formed when the company is established (the decisive moment is the signature of the notarial deed by the founders). A joint-stock company in formation has no legal personality, but has legal identity—it can acquire rights for itself, incur obligations, sue and be sued.

189. The regulations on the joint-stock company apply to a joint-stock company in formation accordingly in matters not otherwise regulated in the CCCP.

190. The name of a joint-stock company in formation should include the additional term “in formation.”

191. A joint-stock company in formation may require the shareholders to contribute ownership rights declared as in-kind contributions.

39. Article 306 CCCP.

192. A joint-stock company in formation operates on the market independently. It can conclude agreements and enter into other legal relationships. Doubts apply to certain types of such relationships. For example, it is not unambiguous whether a joint-stock company in formation may conclude an agreement with the members of its management board, such as an employment contract. This is because a resolution of the general meeting, which does not yet formally exist, is needed for the conclusion of an agreement of this type. Most of the legal doctrine assumes that this is possible.[40]

IV. Number of Subscribers

193. A joint-stock company may be established by one person. This can be either a natural person or a legal person. However, a joint-stock cannot be established solely by a single-person limited liability company. A similar rule applies when establishing limited liability companies. This rule has no special sense—especially given that there is no prohibition on the operation of joint-stock companies in which the sole shareholder is a limited liability company; the prohibition only applies to the process of establishment itself.

194. There is no upper limit to the maximum number of founders and shareholders.

V. Initial Share Capital

195. The share capital of a joint-stock company should be at least PLN 100,000, while the nominal value of the shares may not be less than PLN 0.01.

VI. Contributions in Kind

196. Shares may be taken up in exchange for cash contributions and in exchange for noncash contributions. If noncash contributions are made, the founders must draw up a written report specifying the value of those contributions. This report should be audited by one or several statutory auditors.[41] In principle, the statutory auditor should be appointed by the registry court with jurisdiction over the place of the company's registered office, although it is possible to agree to the auditor appointed by the founders. In the case of a dispute between the founders and the statutory auditor as to the value of the contribution, the registry court will have the deciding vote. No appeal may be filed against the court's decision issued as a result of the motion to consider the application to examine such disputes. However, the registry court may appoint a new statutory auditor if it deems this justified. Certain

40. Cf. K. Bilewska & A. Chłopecki, *Prawo Handlowe*, Warsaw 2019, p. 153.
41. Articles 311 and 312 CCCP.

cash assets, for which the price is known, are not subject to audit by the auditor, including listed securities or assets that have already been audited for the purpose of preparing the financial statements.

VII. Other Material Formation Requirements

197. As indicated above, the emergence of a joint-stock company requires:

- the establishment of the company;
- the provision of contributions by the shareholders to cover the share capital;
- the appointment of a management board and supervisory board and the entry into the register.

198. Additional steps still need to be taken in certain situations.

199. The first additional step of this kind will be the preparation and examination of the founder's report. The need has already been mentioned for the founders to prepare financial statements and to subject them to an audit by a statutory auditor if noncash contributions are made, including mixed contributions, namely consisting partly of a cash contribution and partly of a noncash contribution. The financial statements will also need to be prepared and audited by a statutory auditor if the company acquires property for consideration before registration and if the company pays a fee for services rendered at the time of its establishment.[42]

200. The founders preparing the financial statements referred to above should specify the following in them:[43]

- the subject of the in-kind contributions, as well as the number and type of associated shares or participatory rights issued;
- property and services acquired before registration and the amount and method of payment;
- persons who sold assets to the company, made in-kind contributions or received a fee for services;
- the method used for valuing contributions;
- the appropriate documents confirming the data specified above;
- the justification of the intended transactions.

201. However, if the subject of the contribution or purchase is a business, the financial statements of that business for the last two financial years should be a component of the financial statements of the founders.

42. Article 481 CCCP.
43. Articles 311, 312 CCCP.

202. Finally, in some cases, the establishment of a company requires authorization or its articles of association need to be approved by a competent public authority. This will be the case for banking activities—a bank in the form of a joint-stock company may be established on the basis of a permit from the Polish Financial Supervision Authority.

§3. Essential Elements of the Legal Person: Seat, Name, Objects Clause and (In Some Civil Law Countries—Commercial or Civil) Character

203. The company's seat can be chosen freely, provided that it is located in Poland. The company's seat is a town chosen by the company's founders. This will most frequently be the place where the company's management board operates, but there are no obstacles to choosing a different place, e.g., one where the company has its production plant or plans to do business.

204. The company's seat is of formal significance—for example, in all tax matters, the tax administration authorities encompassing the area in which the company is based will have the jurisdiction. Any possible actions filed against the company should also be filed with the court with jurisdiction over the seat.

205. The name of a joint-stock company may be chosen freely. It should always have the addition "spółka akcyjna" [joint-stock company] or "S.A."

§4. Capital and Shares

I. Different Concepts of Capital

A. *Nominal, Issued, Paid up, Minimum and Authorized Capital (A Subheading for Each)*

1. Nominal

206. The share capital of a joint-stock company is expressed in money of a value which is equal to the sum of the nominal values of the shares.

2. Minimal

207. As mentioned above, the share capital should be at least PLN 100,000. The amount of share capital is specified in the company's articles of association. The change is only possible on the basis of the regulations on increasing or reducing the share capital.

3. Shares

208. The share capital of a joint-stock company is divided into shares. Shares can therefore be treated as part of the share capital corresponding to the quotient of the nominal value of the shares and the value of the share capital.[44]

4. Paid-Up Capital

209. The timing and level of payment for the shares are as follows:

- Shares acquired for in-kind contributions should be paid for before registering the company, at least at a level of a quarter of their nominal value.
- Shares acquired for in-kind contributions should be paid for in whole no later than within one year of the registration of the company.
- If the shares are taken up for in-kind contributions or in-kind contributions and cash simultaneously, the share capital should be covered before registering the company at a level of at least a quarter of its amount.

5. Other Capitals

210. Supplementary capital can also be distinguished in addition to the share capital of a joint-stock company. This capital is obligatory in every joint-stock company. At least 8% of the company's profit for a given financial year is transferred to supplementary capital until the capital reaches at least one-third of the value of the share capital. After the costs of issuing the shares are covered, the share premium should also be transferred to supplementary capital.

211. Reserve capital is also established in a joint-stock company for specific purposes. The articles of association may provide for the establishment of reserves to cover specific losses or expenses. The need to establish reserve capital may also arise from the provisions of the law. An example of this rule will be the need to establish reserve capital equal to the price at which the company purchases its own shares.

II. Alteration of Capital Requirements

212. Capital can be increased and decreased in joint-stock companies. An increase in capital is a special type of amendment to the articles of association. There are extensive rules for increasing the level of share capital.

---

44. Cf. A. Koch & J. Napierała, *Prawo* ... , p. 476.

213. An ordinary increase in the share capital, an increase in capital based on the target capital, and a conditional increase in the share capital can be distinguished in a joint-stock company.

214. From the technical point of view, the share capital is increased by issuing new shares, increasing the nominal value of the existing shares or issuing new shares combined with increasing the value of previously issued shares.

215. New shares may be issued through a private placement, a closed subscription or an open subscription. The first of these involves the company making an offer to a specific recipient, who accepts the offer. The second involves offering shares exclusively to the shareholders. After all, the shareholders have the preemptive right to acquire shares in the increased share capital. In turn, an open subscription involves addressing the offer to persons who are not entitled to a preemptive right, including third parties.

216. Issuing new shares alone does not yet lead to an increase in the level of share capital. The shares from the new issue need to be acquired by existing or new shareholders. In most cases, the level of share capital is merely formally increased when the increase is registered.

III. Preferential Right of Subscription

217. The shareholders have the preemptive right to acquire the new shares in proportion to the number of shares already held. The Polish legal doctrine distinguishes between the abstract priority right to acquire new shares, which is treated as an element of the shareholder's right to a share and the specific preemptive right, namely the shareholder's claim on the company for the allocation of a specific number of shares from the specific, new issue. This last right is a transferable property right, a security.

218. Preemptive rights enable shareholders to maintain their current balance of power in the company within the general meeting, regardless of the new share issue. They can also prevent the reduction of the value of their shares (their dilution).

219. It is admissible to rule out the preemptive right, although this requires a decision of the general meeting, which may be made if this is justified by the company's interests. A resolution of the general meeting to deprive shareholders of their preemptive rights requires a majority of at least four-fifths of the votes.

IV. Issues of Shares at a Premium and at a Discount

220. If the shares are acquired at a premium (agio), the premium should be paid in full before registering the company.

V. Public Issue Requirements (Prospectuses) and Promoters

221. In Polish law, capital market law is distinguished as a separate legal discipline. This area is a conglomeration of norms of civil, administrative and criminal law. The matter regarding a public joint-stock company is largely based on the provisions of the CCCP regarding all other joint-stock companies, but supplementing these regulations with their own, specific principles.

222. According to Polish law, any joint-stock company, in which at least one share is dematerialized in the meaning of the regulations on trading in financial instruments, is treated as a public company. On Western capital markets, a public company is most frequently a company listed on a stock exchange or a multilateral trading facility. The Polish definition is incorrect and rightly criticized in the legal doctrine.[45]

223. The procedure for selling the shares of a public company differs from the procedure for selling shares of other companies. The two main ways of selling public companies are primary trading and an initial public offering (IPO). Primary trading means acquiring a new issue of shares, the result of which is the creation of these shares. However, the IPO is the first sale of already issued, acquired and registered shares. The largest IPOs in Poland in the last two decades were the sale of shares in the largest private Polish entities, previously operating as state-owned enterprises. However, the State Treasury very frequently retained control over these companies, including after the IPO.

224. Shares are offered through brokerage houses. The offerors are the entity selling its shares, as well as the brokerage house that organizes a consortium for selling securities. The offering is based on a sales prospectus that is approved by the Polish Financial Supervision Authority. There is no need to prepare one in some cases. An information memorandum is prepared in cases in which the scope of information that is to be provided is smaller than at the initial offering of the shares, as in the case of a new issue of shares in a public company.

225. Shares are offered through an investment company.

226. The issue sponsor organizes the consortium, which collects subscriptions for the shares of a public company and draws up a list on the basis of which the shares are recorded on securities accounts. All the elements, which are normally associated with public accounts, such as due diligence, book building, roadshow, underwriting, etc., appear in practice. However, the reservation is that Polish law distinguishes only two types of underwriting—investment underwriting and service underwriting. The former involves the acquisition of the shares not acquired in the offering, while the latter assumes the acquisition of all shares from a further issue and further sales (e.g., within management options) which, even so, is treated as an IPO.

---

45. Cf. K. Bilewska & A. Chłopecki, *Prawo Handlowe,* p. 223.

227. A public company's shares are allocated according to the rules set out in the sales prospectus. The management board conducts the allocation.

228. Polish law also admits the Green shoe option mechanism.

VI. Stock Exchange Introduction Requirements

229. A joint-stock company, which is a public company, is subject to additional requirements that apply to such entities. This had been regulated in the provisions of the capital market and partly also in the general provisions of commercial law. The provisions regulating the public company are treated as specific acts with respect to the general regulation on the joint-stock company. There are sometimes inaccuracies at the point of interconnection between the regulations on private companies and the regulations on public companies. An example will be the regulation on the information obligations, where the general regulations awarding specific rights to all shareholders of joint-stock companies coexist with the regulations on the capital market, which regulate the obligation to provide current information, regular information and important information affecting the price to the public, whereby the last of this information is insider information. The information duties of public companies primarily arise from the principle of equal access to information by all investors in that company, both current and potential, regardless of whether they are larger or smaller investors.

230. A public joint-stock company has specific rules regarding the general meeting. For instance, shareholders of a public company representing at least one-twentieth of the company's share capital may submit draft resolutions on matters introduced into the agenda of the general meeting or matters which may be introduced into the meeting agenda to the company in writing or electronically. The company should post such draft resolutions on its website to enable the largest possible group of addressees to read them. The announcement should be posted at least twenty-six days before the date of the general meeting.

231. The general meeting of every joint-stock company may be held in Warsaw.

232. The key difference between an ordinary joint-stock company and a public joint-stock company is the specification of the right to participate in the general meeting. The shareholders at a given moment are entitled to participate in the general meeting of a private company. In the case of public companies, anyone who was a shareholder in the company sixteen days before the date of the general meeting is entitled to participate in the general meeting of such companies. This date is the date of registration of participation in the general meeting. A shareholder of a public company may sell his shares between the date on which his participation in the general meeting is registered and the date on which the general meeting ends. However, the Polish legal doctrine is unclear as to whether a shareholder, who sells his shares in the period between the date of registering his participation in the general meeting and the date of the end of the general meeting, can vote on shares that he no longer owns. Can such a shareholder object to a resolution of the general meeting? According to some authors, this is unacceptable, because it would be systemically in conflict with the linguistic interpretation.[46] However, it appears that this view is systemically incorrect and it should rather be accepted that such persons can have and actually have the right to behave as shareholders at the general meeting of a public company.

233. Further separate regulations of a public company apply to the different regulations of pledges on shares. The establishment of a pledge on dematerialized shares requires the account to be blocked, so since the shares are on the shareholder's account, it is he and not the pledgee, who may exercise the right to vote, which is associated with them.

234. A public joint-stock company may also not issue new shares with a preference with regard to voting. However, it may have preference shares with regard to voting if these shares were issued at a time when the company was not yet a public company. Companies with shares that actually have a preference operate on the Warsaw Stock Exchange.

235. In the case of the supervisory board—the supervisory board of a public company consists of at least five members, in contrast with at least three members of the supervisory board of a private company.

236. In a public company, a shareholder may also vote as a proxy when passing resolutions concerning him, which is prohibited in private companies.

237. A squeeze-out is also regulated slightly differently. In particular, a demand may be sent to all other shareholders to sell all their shares after exceeding 90% of the total number of votes in a given company. In private companies, a squeeze-out is only possible after exceeding 95% of the share capital.

238. In the case of a public company, the deadline for filing an action to repeal a resolution of that general meeting has been further shortened from six months to three months from the date on which the resolution is passed.

VII. Forbidden Reductions of Capital and Acquisition of Shares by the Corporation Itself

A. Acquisition of Shares by the Corporation Itself

239. In principle, a joint-stock company cannot acquire shares which it issued. The law simultaneously provides for several exceptions to this prohibition. The most important of these are:

46. Cf. K. Bilewska & A. Chłopecki, *Prawo Handlowe*, p. 240.

- the acquisition of shares to prevent serious damage with which the company is directly threatened;
- the acquisition of shares to be offered to the employees or persons employed by the company or an affiliate for purchase for at least three years;
- a public company acquiring shares to fulfill its obligations arising from debt instruments that are convertible into shares;
- the acquisition of shares through universal succession, e.g., in the case of inheritance;
- a financial institution that acquires fully paid-up shares on someone else's account for the purpose of resale;
 the acquisition of shares to redeem them;
- the acquisition of fully paid-up shares through enforcement to satisfy the company's claims, which cannot be otherwise satisfied from the shareholder's assets;
- the acquisition of fully paid-up shares free of charge;
- acquisition on the basis and within the limits of the authorization granted by the general meeting—such authorization should specify the terms and conditions of the acquisition, including the maximum number of shares to be acquired, the authorization period (maximum of five years), and the maximum and minimum amount of payment for the shares purchased.

240. The acquisition of the company's own shares may be audited. In particular, the management board is required to notify the next general meeting of the reasons or objective of acquiring ownership, the number and nominal value of these shares, their share of the share capital and the value of the performance fulfilled with the shares.

241. As a rule, the company's own shares which it acquires should be sold within a year of the date of their acquisition by the company or offered to employees or other persons within this period. In some cases, this period is two years.

242. The company does not conduct share work on its own shares.

243. A company may not subscribe for the shares of its subsidiary company or cooperative.

B. *Financing of the Acquisition or the Purchase of Its Shares by the Corporation*

244. After certain conditions are satisfied, Polish law allows for the direct or indirect financing of the acquisition or subscription for shares issued by the company. This can be performed through a loan granted by the company, an advance or the establishment of collateral. Therefore, a company may finance the acquisition or subscription for the shares it issues. However, in order to do this, reserve capital should be established for the amount to be assigned for allocation among the shareholders.

245. A resolution of the general meeting will need to be passed for the company to be able to finance the acquisition of or subscription for the shares it is issuing. The resolution is passed on the basis of a written report from the management board. In the report, the management board should specify the reasons for or the objective of the financing, the company's interest in financing, the terms and conditions of the financing and the financing risk in terms of liquidity and solvency of the company, as well as the acquisition or subscription price.

246. The company may only finance the acquisition of or subscription for its shares on market conditions. The simplified requirements only apply to performances for the company's or its affiliate's employees, the objective of which is to facilitate the acquisition of or subscription for the shares issued by the company.

C. Reduction of Share Capital

247. The reduction of the share capital requires a special amendment to the articles of association. A reduction in the share capital is combined with a reduction in the nominal value of the shares or a reduction in the number of shares through their redemption or a merger of shares. Apart from the reduction in the share capital, shares can also be canceled in isolation of a reduction of the share capital, in which case the value of the shares is paid for out of net profit.

248. The resolution to reduce the share capital should specify the objective of the reduction, the amount by which the share capital is to be reduced and the method of reduction.

249. The share capital cannot be reduced below the minimum value of the share capital, which, in a joint-stock company, is PLN 100,000. Additionally, a reduction in the nominal value of the shares cannot result in the emergence of shares of a value of less than PLN 0.01.

250. The share capital is reduced by paying out an amount to the shareholders or transferring out the amount to share capital—as a result of which the share capital is reduced in the balance sheet, while there are no real asset consequences for the company because the money that was in the company is still there.

251. In the event of the intention to reduce the share capital, this fact must be disclosed externally to enable the company's creditors to possibly report their claims. These claims should be reported within three months of the date on which the company announces that the company's general meeting passed a resolution on the reduction in the share capital. Creditors may also demand that their claims, which are not yet due and which arose before the announcement of the resolution on the reduction in the share capital, are secured if it is likely that the reduction in the share capital will pose a threat to the satisfaction of the claims reported by these creditors, and these claims are not secured by the company.

252. There is no need to announce the resolutions on the reduction in the share capital in several cases. Among other things, when, despite reducing the share capital, the capital contributions paid by the shareholders are not returned to them or these shareholders are not exempted from making capital contributions, at the same time as the reduction in the share capital, the capital is simultaneously increased by means of a new issue, the shares from which will be fully paid up. Additionally, if the reduction in the share capital has the objective of compensating for losses suffered or of transferring specific amounts to reserve capital, the reduction in the share capital does not need to be announced. An announcement will also not be required if the share capital is reduced as a result of a cancellation of the company's shares, which were not sold within the expected deadline, by way of a resolution of the management board.

VIII. Classes of Shares

A. Bearer-Nominative

253. The general rules for shares are as follows:

- every share must have a nominal value specified in the articles of association, which corresponds to the quotient of the value of the share capital and the number of shares;[47]
- the value of the shares must be equal to the nominal value;[48]
- the nominal value of the shares may not be lower than PLN 0.01;[49]
- the nominal value of the shares may be changed by amending the company's articles of association when increasing the capital, by increasing the nominal value of the shares or reducing the capital by reducing the nominal value of the shares[50] and by dividing the shares, namely by increasing the number of shares without changing the value of the share capital.

B. Preferred Stock

254. In principle, the scope of rights from shares to which a shareholder is entitled with respect to the company depends on the number and type of shares he holds. In the case of ordinary shares, each of them gives the same rights. This also arises from the principle of equal treatment of shareholders and the principle of proportionality of contributions and rights in a joint-stock company, which are applicable under Polish law.

47. Article 304 §1, item 5 CCCP.
48. Article 302 CCCP.
49. Article 308 §2 CCCP.
50. Article 432 §1 and Art. 455 §1 CCCP.

255. However, the CCCP also allows for shares and special rights, namely preference shares, to be issued. Examples of preferred types have been listed directly in the regulations. The preference of the shares may apply, in particular, to voting rights, the right to a dividend or the distribution of assets in the case of the liquidation of a joint-stock company. However, other preferences not explicitly mentioned are also possible, such as preference in terms of preemptive rights, priority in the redemption of shares, the right to recover in-kind contributions, etc. The general framework only imposes a prohibition on granting preference that would be in conflict with the nature of a joint-stock company or good practices.

256. Only registered shares can be preferred.

C. Deferred

257. A deferred share is a share that does not have any rights to the assets of a company undergoing bankruptcy until all common and preferred shareholders are paid. Polish law does not recognize this type of share as a special type of share.

D. Non-voting

258. Polish law allows for silent shares to be issued. They can be either bearer shares or registered shares. Silent shares may be traded on the stock exchange. The condition for issuing silent shares is their preference in terms of the dividend. A silent share must therefore always be a preference share with regard to the dividend. Lifting the preferences of silent shares results in the shareholder gaining the right to vote with such shares.

E. Multiple Voting

259. Polish law allows for preference shares with regard to voting rights to be issued. The maximum number of votes per share may not exceed two votes. Therefore, it would be inadmissible, for instance, to grant the shareholder the right to object to certain resolutions of the general meeting.[51]

F. Certificate and Warrant Shares

260. Share options and futures contracts, as well as subscription warrants, constitute so-called derivative rights. A share option includes a right arising as a result of an issue building the rights to acquire or subscribe for securities. The holder of share options has the right to demand that the issuer of the option either sell the

---

51. *See also* A. Koch & J. Napierała, *Prawo …*, p. 502.

shares to him or that the issuer buy the shares from him at a predetermined price on or up to a specified date. The issuer of the option receives payment in the form of a bonus in exchange for the readiness to sell or buy shares. The holder of the option may or may not exercise his right.

261. In trading practice, forward contracts operate in such a way that the effect of the option holder exercising the right is that the difference between the price set in the contract and the market price is entered into the account.

262. The legal classification of options is disputed under Polish law—some authors believe that an option is the right to unilaterally establish a relationship of a sale or purchase of shares. Others believe that it is the right to demand the conclusion of a contract for the sale or purchase of the shares.

263. In turn, under a forward contract, one party undertakes to buy a specific financial instrument, e.g., shares, while the other party undertakes to sell at a certain time, at a predetermined price. The difference between forward contracts and stock options is that both parties are required to exercise a forward contract.

264. The subscription warrants referred to in Article 453 §2 of the CCCP are securities issued by a joint-stock company, registered or bearer securities giving the holder the right to subscribe for or acquire shares in that company, excluding pre-emptive rights. A resolution of the general meeting must be passed in order to issue a subscription warrant, which specifies the persons who are entitled to subscribe for warrants, the issue price of the warrants or the method of setting it and the number of shares per warrant.

G. Free Shares

265. Free shares are issued to shareholders if the share capital is increased with the company's own funds, such as a reserve fund or supplementary fund.[52] In such a situation, the shareholders receive free shares because they do not make contributions in exchange for their shares. The shareholders acquire the free shares in proportion to the shares already held in the share capital.

H. Restricted Shares

266. Restricted shares are such shares in which the sale is contractually limited. Polish law allows for the ability to conclude agreements restricting the disposal of shares for a certain time. However, this is only effective between the parties.

52. Article 442 §3 CCCP.

IX. Transfer of Shares

A. *Registration*

267. Shares are transferable. This general rule can only be restricted in certain situations and very precisely. The restrictions can only apply to registered shares. Various types of restrictions are possible, for example, a restriction may be introduced into the articles of association such that the company needs to grant permission for the sale of the shares. Other ways of limiting the sale of registered shares include the award of the right of first refusal on the acquisition of shares by existing shareholders, restrictions for persons with specific qualifications, territorial restrictions, etc.

268. If the restriction of marketability involves the need to obtain permission from the company, this permission is granted by the management board in writing, unless otherwise arises from the articles of association. If the company refuses to give permission to sell the shares, it needs to specify another buyer.

269. Polish law also allows for the conclusion of agreements establishing restrictions on the transferability of shares, such as preemption rights, options or other rights of first refusal to acquire shares.

270. Shares are transferred by a written declaration on the share itself or in a separate document—in the case of registered shares. However, bearer shares are sold by transferring the shares. The price needs to be paid in all cases.

B. *Gift-Sale*

271. Polish law does not have specific rules on this.

C. *Stock Exchange*

272. In the case of dematerialized securities, rights to given securities are transferred when the respective entry is made on the securities account. However, an agreement may be concluded that contains an obligation to sell the securities before they are entered into the buyer's securities account.

D. *Protection of Shareholders in Case of Tender Offer*

273. Directive 2004/109/EC of the European Parliament and of the Council of December 15, 2004, on the harmonization of transparency requirements in relation to information about issuers whose securities are admitted to trading on a regulated market, as well as the rules arising from the Transparency Directive (2001/34/EC) and Directive 2004/25/EC of the European Parliament and of the Council of April 21, 2004, on takeover bids have been implemented into Polish law.

274. The acquisition of large blocks of shares in public companies encompasses two groups of situations. The first is the situation related to the emergence of the information duty, namely the disclosure of the ownership of shares. The second is a situation related to the obligation to offer the shareholders to buy back their shares by way of a call.

275. The information obligations are activated by exceeding a certain threshold or falling below a certain threshold. These thresholds are as follows: 5%, 10%, 15%, 20%, 25%, 33%, 50%, 75%, and 90% of the total number of votes in a public company. An entity that exceeds such a threshold, or which increases its ownership or reduces its ownership by passing through a group is required to notify the Polish Financial Supervision Authority and the issuer forthwith. He should do this within four business days of the date on which he learned about the change in the share of the total number of votes. In the case of the acquisition of shares in a public company on a regulated market, the notification should be sent within six trading days of the date of the transaction. The company makes such information public.

276. In addition, information obligations arise when the share held to date of over 10% of the total number of votes changes by at least 2% of the total number of votes.

277. However, a call, namely the obligation to propose to the shareholders the acquisition of the shares they hold, must be made in two situations. First, when a number of shares in a public company is to be acquired which increases the share of the total number of votes by more than 10% of the total number of votes within a period of less than sixty days, by an entity with less than 33% of the total number of votes in that company.

278. Second, when a number of shares in a public company is to be acquired, which increases the share of the total number of votes by more than 5% of the total number of votes in a period of less than twelve months, by a shareholder holding at least 33% of the total number of votes in that company.

279. Additionally, in the case of exceeding 33% or 66% of the total number of votes in a public company, a call must also be announced for 100% of the shares if the threshold of 33% of the number of votes may be exceeded on a number of shares giving up to 66% of votes. Meanwhile, if 66% of the number of votes is exceeded, only a call on 100% of the remaining shares can be made.

280. If the threshold of 33% or 66% of the total number of votes in a public company is exceeded as a result of events which were beyond the shareholder's control, for example, in the case of inheritance, the shareholder has three months to dispose of the shares to a level that is below the threshold if he does not want to announce a call, or he needs to announce a call.

281. As pointed out in the legal doctrine, the threshold of 66% differs from the threshold, which is usually specified in other European regulations. This is important because, in the formal sense, control over the company is usually acquired after the acquisition of 50% of the number of votes and, in the event of a dispersed shareholding, even with a smaller number of votes.[53] According to the representatives of the Polish legal doctrine, such a regulation arises from the fact that the Polish lawmakers give primacy to the capital market as a whole instead of to the minority shareholders. This, in turn, arises from the fact that, unlike in countries with a longer history, Poland has a much greater dispersion of the shareholding.

282. The call should be made through a brokerage house; it should specify the minimum price of the call, which should be set in compliance with the requirements arising from the provisions of the law.

283. The obligations regarding the call are also applicable when shares in a given company are held by more than one person, but the persons or entities are related to each other (action in concert).

284. If the above thresholds are reached or exceeded in breach of the disclosure obligations, the shareholder may not exercise voting rights from the shares in the public company.

E. Insider Trading

285. Polish law contains rules prohibiting insider trading, which are similar to those in most Western countries.

286. In the Polish legal framework, the offense of insider trading is customarily referred to as using and disclosing confidential information.

287. The underlying law concerning protecting the market from unlawful abuse of confidential information is currently Regulation (EU) No. 596/2014 of the European Parliament and of the Council of April 16, 2014, on market abuse (market abuse regulation) and repealing Directive 2003/6/EC of the European Parliament and of the Council and Commission Directives 2003/124/EC, 2003/125/EC and 2004/72/EC (the so-called MAR Regulation). The subject matter of that law is, among other things, creating a common regulatory framework for using and unlawfully disclosing confidential information. The MAR Regulation is characterized by its directly binding effect.

288. The European legislator also deemed it necessary to penalize, if committed willfully, the most severe cases of using confidential information, making recommendations to another or soliciting them to use confidential information. The Member States were obliged to do so by Directive 2014/57/EU of the European

53. Cf. K. Bilewska & A. Chłopecki, *Prawo Handlowe*, p. 236.

Parliament and of the Council of April 16, 2014, on criminal sanctions for market abuse (Market Abuse Directive) (the so-called MAD II Directive).

289. In the Polish legal framework, criminalization of confidential information abuse has been effected in Articles 179–182 of the Act on trading in financial instruments of November 29, 2005. They are umbrella regulations and they refer to the provisions of Regulation 596/2021 and Regulation 648/2012.[54]

290. As provided for in the abovementioned act, confidential information has been defined in Article 3 item 52, though this provision refers to Article 7 paragraph 1 letter a of the MAR Regulation featuring a more extensive definition of the term. Pursuant to the abovementioned provision, confidential information comprises information of a precise nature, which has not been made public, relating, directly or indirectly, to one or more issuers or to one or more financial instruments, and which, if it were made public, would be likely to have a significant effect on the prices of those financial instruments or on the price of related derivative financial instruments.

291. As provided for in Article 179a of the Act, anyone who, in breach of the obligation set forth in Article 28 paragraph 4, Article 33 paragraph 5, Article 83 or Article 84 of Regulation 648/2012, discloses confidential information as defined in said Regulation or uses such information for purposes other than those set forth in said Regulation shall be subject to a fine of up to PLN 1 million or incarceration of up to three years, or both.

292. The offense of confidential information abuse referred to in Article 179a is of an individual nature. It may only be committed by the individuals to whom the obligations listed therein apply.

293. Pursuant to Article 180 of the Act, anyone who, contrary to the prohibition referred to in Article 14 letter c of Regulation 596/2014, discloses confidential information shall be subject to a fine of up to PLN 2 million or incarceration of up to four years, or both.

294. Pursuant to Article 181 of the Act, anyone who, contrary to the prohibition referred to in Article 14 letter a of Regulation 596/2014, uses confidential information shall be subject to a fine of up to PLN 5 million or incarceration of between three months to five years, or both.

295. Pursuant to Article 182 of the Act, anyone who, contrary to the prohibition referred to in Article 14 letter b of Regulation 596/2014, makes a recommendation to another or solicits them to acquire or dispose of financial instruments to which

54. P. Binas [w:] *Prawo karne gospodarcze, red. R. Zawłocki, System Prawa Handlowego* [eng. P Binas [in:] *Commercial Penal Law, Et al. R. Zawłocki, Commercial Law System*], volume 10, Warszawa 2018, pp. 654–655.

confidential information pertains shall be subject to a fine of up to PLN 2 million or incarceration of up to four years, or both.

296. The offenses referred to in Articles 180–182 of the Act are of a general nature, which arises directly from Article 14 of Regulation 596/2014. Pursuant to this provision, all individuals are prohibited from: (a) using or attempting to use confidential information; (b) making recommendations to another or soliciting them to use confidential information; (c) unlawfully disclosing confidential information.

297. The objective of the provisions penalizing confidential information abuse is to ensure that trading in financial instruments is secure and that access to confidential information is equal and nondiscriminatory to all capital market participants. To that end, the obligation, provided for in the MAR Regulation, to immediately publish confidential information[55] has been imposed.

X. (Mortgage) Debentures and Other Securities Which Do Not (Yet) Represent Capital

298. Polish law recognizes a whole series of securities related to shares in organized trading. These include:

- Rights to shares.
- Depositary receipts.
- Convertible bonds and bonds with preemptive rights.
- Preemptive rights.
- Derivative rights incorporating the right to purchase or subscribe for shares.
- Subscription warrants.

299. The right to shares is a security giving the right, which is not in the form of a document, to receive shares in a new public company, which arises at the time of allotment of these shares and expires upon the registration of the shares in the securities depository or on the date on which the registration court's decision refusing to enter the increase in the share capital increase in the register of entrepreneurs becomes final.[56]

300. In turn, a depositary receipt enables a public company with its registered office in Poland to introduce shares onto the market of another country and a company which has a registered office in another country to introduce shares on the Polish market. Therefore, a depositary receipt embodies the right to shares and shares of a company which has its registered office in a country other than that of the registered office of the issuer of the depositary receipt.

55. Article 17, para. 1 of MAR.
56. Article 3, item 29 of the Act on trading in financial instruments.

301. In turn, convertible bonds are bonds that entitle bondholders to subscribe for shares in exchange for bonds, while bonds with preemptive rights entitle bondholders to subscribe for shares in the company with priority over its shareholders. The exercise of bondholders' rights is ensured by the institution of a conditional increase in share capital.[57]

302. The preemptive right is a priority right to subscribe for new shares with respect to the number of shares held. Preemptive rights to shares of a specific issue may be independently traded.[58]

303. The last three items in this category, namely share options and forward contracts, as well as subscription warrants, have been discussed above.

§5. Shareholders, Management and Control

I. Shareholder Control Mechanisms/Shareholders

A. Shareholders Meeting (Kinds, Convening, Proxies, Powers)

304. The general meeting is the company's ownership body.

305. Shareholders, pledgees and users of shares are entitled to participate in a general meeting of private companies.

306. Shareholders have the right to attend meetings if they have submitted bearer share documents to the company at least one week before the date of the meeting (in the case of shareholders holding bearer shares) or those who have been entered into the register of shareholders at least one week before the general meeting (in the case of shareholders of registered shares and temporary certificates).

307. However, three categories of entities have the right to participate in the general meeting of a public company:

- First, those entitled to dematerialized shares, who have the status of shareholders of a public company sixteen days before the date of the general meeting.
- Second, the holders of bearer shares, if they submit their share documents no later than on the date of registration of their participation in the general meeting of shareholders.
- Third, those entitled to registered shares and temporary certificates, as well as pledgees and users who are entitled to vote, if they are entered into the register of shareholders on the date of registration at the general meeting.

---

57. Article 448 CCCP.
58. Cf. A. Koch & J. Napierała, *Prawo* … , p. 518 and A. Szumański (in:) *System prawa prywatnego T.16* [eng. *System of Private Law, Volume 16*], A. Szajkowski ed., p. 194.

308. As demonstrated above, some authors of the Polish legal doctrine believe that the holder of shares in a public company loses the right to participate in the general meeting of shareholders on the date of registration, if they were to sell their shares before the end of that general meeting.[59] These authors make the assumption that only shareholders are entitled to participate in a general meeting.

309. Shareholders are not obliged to attend a general meeting.

310. Shareholders may exercise their rights through proxies. The power of attorney to participate in the voting at the general meeting of a nonpublic company must be in writing in order to be valid.[60] However, in a public company, an ordinary written form or an unqualified electronic form is required. Members of the management board and employees of the company cannot be proxies in a nonpublic company.

311. A proxy may grant a further power of attorney if this right arises from the wording of the power of attorney.

312. A proxy may represent more than one shareholder and vote differently with the shares of each shareholder.

313. Members of the management board and the supervisory board also have the right to participate in a general meeting—obviously without the right to vote.

314. Polish law distinguishes between two types of general meetings. These are the annual general meeting and the extraordinary general meeting.

315. An annual general meeting must be called once a year within six months of the end of each financial year. A vote of approach is given at the annual general meeting to the members of the management board and the supervisory board for the performance of their duties in the previous year and the financial statements are approved.

316. General meetings are called by the management board. They may be called by the supervisory board if the management board fails to call it within the deadline prescribed by law or in the statutory regulations. The supervisory board may also call an extraordinary general meeting on its own initiative. It may also be called by shareholders representing at least half the share capital or at least half of the total number of votes in the company. The articles of association may also grant other persons the right to call a general meeting. Finally, shareholders representing at least

59. Cf. A. Chłopecki, *Materialnoprawne i legitymacyjne skutki tak zwanego record date* [eng. *Substantive Law and Legitimation Effects of the So-Called Record Date*], PPH 2010, No. 6, pp. 22–26; M. Michalski, *Reżim legitymacyjny w spółce akcyjnej* [eng. *Legitimation Regime in a Joint-Stock Company*], PPH 2011, No. 2, pp. 23–30 and A. Koch & J. Napierała, *Prawo …*, p. 565.

60. Article 412^1 §1 CCCP.

one-twentieth of the share capital may request that an extraordinary general meeting be called. The articles of association may grant the right to demand that an extraordinary general meeting be called to shareholders who represent less than one-twentieth of the share capital.

317. In the case of nonpublic companies, the fact that a general meeting is called should be announced in the official journal, Monitor Sądowy i Gospodarczy and in the magazine intended for the company's announcements at least three weeks before the date of the meeting, unless all the company's shares are registered, in which case the general meeting may also be called by email if the shareholders have given their prior consent for this. However, the fact that a public company's general meeting has been called should be posted on the company's website and through a current report.

318. In small joint-stock companies, resolutions of the general meeting may also be passed without the meeting being formally called, including on matters not on the agenda.[61] This is possible when the whole of the share capital is represented at the general meeting, and, simultaneously, none of the attendees object to the general meeting being held.

319. The general meeting is held at the company's registered office and, in the case of listed companies, also in Warsaw.

320. The list of shareholders entitled to participate in the general meeting should be displayed at the management board's premises for three weekdays before the date of the general meeting. This list should include the number of votes to which each such individual is entitled.

321. The general meeting is opened by the chairman of the supervisory board or his deputy unless otherwise arises from the provisions of the CCCP or the provisions of the articles of association.

B. Majority Rule: Legal and Statutory Protection of Minority and Majority

322. In principle, the general meeting will be valid in the case of joint-stock companies regardless of the number of shares represented. The regulations only introduce a requirement of a quorum in some cases. For example, for a resolution to be passed on an issue not included in the meeting agenda, the whole of the share capital must be represented at the meeting; in the case of passing a resolution preventing the dissolution of the company, the presence of at least half of the share capital is required.

323. Voting in joint-stock companies is generally public. Secret ballots are only required in some cases. Polish courts take the view that a breach of the obligation

61. Article 405 and Art. 404 CCCP.

to order a secret ballot has or may have such a significant impact on the outcome of the voting that the mere fact that the rule of the secret ballot is breached is a sufficient basis for successfully appealing against a resolution of the general meeting.[62] Such voting applies to:

(1) voting on appointments and on motions to dismiss members of the company's governing bodies;
(2) voting on motions to bring members of the company's governing bodies or liquidators to justice;
(3) in voting on personnel matters;
(4) and in every vote at the request of at least one of the shareholders present or represented at the general meeting.

324. In principle, resolutions are passed with an absolute majority of votes cast. This means that more than half of the votes are cast in favor. Abstentions actually count as votes against.

325. The articles of association may introduce different requirements regarding the required majority of votes. However, in the legal doctrine, some authors consider that the introduction of a hypothetical requirement of unanimity in passing all resolutions would breach the nature of a joint-stock company.[63] It is inadmissible to relax the requirements in situations where a provision of the Act unconditionally provides for a qualified majority.[64]

326. A qualified majority of two-thirds of the votes is required, among others, for:

(1) a resolution on the purchase of property for the company for a price of over one-tenth of the founder's or shareholder's paid-up share capital or from a parent or subsidiary company;
(2) a resolution on a material change in the company's activities;
(3) a resolution on the company's financing of the acquisition of or subscription for shares.

327. In turn, the following resolutions are among those requiring three-quarters of the votes:

(1) a resolution regarding the issue of convertible bonds and bonds with preemptive rights to subscribe for shares, amendments to the articles of association, the redemption of shares, the reduction of the share capital and the sale of an enterprise;

---

62. Cf. Supreme Court's judgment of May 26, 1990, III CKN 261/98, PS 2000/4, pp. 39–44; and A. Koch & J. Napierała, *Prawo* ... , p. 571.
63. Cf., A. Koch & J. Napierała, *Prawo* ... , p. 572.
64. Cf. J. Frąckowiak (in:) *Kodeks spółek handlowych. Komentarz* [eng. *Code of Commercial Companies and Partnerships. Commentary*], K. Kruczalak (ed.), p. 669.

(2) a resolution on the transformation of a joint-stock company into another company;
(3) a resolution on increasing the share capital (in certain cases).

328. However, the following resolutions are among those that require a four-fifths majority of votes:

(1) resolutions depriving shareholders of the preemptive right to a new share issue; and
(2) a resolution disabling the preemptive right to convertible securities.

329. The will of a 95% majority of votes is required for resolutions regarding a so-called squeeze-out, namely squeezing out minority shareholders by forcing the acquisition of their shares. It should be emphasized that shareholders of a public company are not entitled to remove a minority from the company.

330. The right to conduct a squeeze-out involves the ability of the general meeting to pass a resolution on the compulsory buyout of shares from shareholders representing no more than 5% of the share capital. Such a buyout of shares may be made by no more than five shareholders holding a total of no less than 95% of the share capital, each holding no less than 5% of the share capital. The resolution of the general meeting should contain a plan for the purchase of the shares. Interestingly, the shareholders who are to acquire shares and vote for the resolution, are jointly and severally liable to the company for paying the entire buyout amount (second sentence of Article 408 §2 of the CCCP). The shares are bought back by the management board on behalf of the majority shareholders.

331. In turn, the consent of all the shareholders to whom the resolution applies is necessary when passing a resolution amending the company's articles of association, if this is an amendment to the articles of association increasing the benefits of the shareholders and if the change in status applies to the reduction of the rights conferred personally to individual shareholders.

332. And finally, resolutions may only be passed on matters not included in the agenda and if the general meeting is not formally called, if two conditions are jointly satisfied. First, the whole of the share capital is represented at that general meeting. And second, none of those present objected to passing a resolution or the general meeting being held or the inclusion of specific matters on the agenda.

C. Annual Account and Report; Profits and Dividends

333. Polish law distinguishes between the abstract right to a share of the profit and a shareholder's claims on the company after the disbursement of the share of profit assigned to him for distribution.

334. A shareholder cannot be deprived of the right to participate in the distribution of the profit. However, it is possible that in one or more subsequent years, the shareholder will not receive a dividend. This will be the case if the company fails to make a profit or if the profit generated is not intended for distribution to the shareholders.

335. It is inadmissible to transfer or encumber the right to participate in the distribution of the profit without reallocating the shares. However, a shareholder is able to manage/dispose of claims for the payment of a specific dividend. It has also been accepted in the legal doctrine that a shareholder is able to manage/dispose of a future claim, namely for the payment of a future dividend.[65] No disputes are pending with respect to the latter issue.

336. The method of distributing profit should be specified in the articles of association. Unless otherwise arises from the articles of association, the profit for distribution should be evenly divided among the number of shares if the shares have been fully paid up, whereas if the shares have not been fully paid up, the distribution should be evenly divided proportionally to the payments made per share.

337. The shareholders also have the ability to participate in the company's profits during the financial year by receiving advances on dividends.

338. It will only be possible to make an advance towards the dividend if all of the following conditions are satisfied:

- The management board has been authorized in the articles of association to make advance payments (first sentence of Article 349 §1 of the CCCP).
- The financial statements for the previous financial year approved by the general meeting disclose a profit (first sentence of Article 349 §2 of the CCCP).
- The supervisory board approved the advance payment (second sentence of Article 349 §1 of the CCCP).
- The company has sufficient funds to make the payment (first sentence of Article 349 §1 of the CCCP).

339. The advance payment may not be greater than the amount of profit generated since the end of the financial year plus the reserve capital established from profit but reduced by unrealized accumulated losses and the company's own shares.

D. Supervisory Board

340. The supervisory board is an obligatory body in every Polish joint-stock company. Polish law is of the position that ownership should be strictly separated from control over the company. The company is controlled precisely by the supervisory board.

---

65. Cf. A. Koch & J. Napierała, *Prawo* ... , p. 485.

341. In nonpublic companies, it consists of at least three members. However, in public companies, it has a minimum of two to five people. Within the internal organization of the supervisory board of a joint-stock company, one of its members holds the post of chairman. A deputy chairman and secretary may also be appointed.

342. The supervisory boards of larger companies may also appoint a committee within the supervisory board. The most frequently appointed committees are the audit committee and the salaries committee. In some cases, the appointment of an audit committee is obligatory.

343. Supervisory board members are appointed and dismissed by the general meeting unless otherwise arises from the company's articles of association.

344. A member of the management board, a prosecutor, a liquidator or a person employed at the company as the chief accountant, a legal counsel or an attorney-at-law cannot be a member of the supervisory board.

345. Polish law also contains detailed guidelines on the possibilities of electing a supervisory board. The rules are designed to protect the interests of the minority shareholders. This applies to the avoidance of a situation in which a majority shareholder appoints all the members of the supervisory board. These rules are based on the fact that, at the request of a shareholder holding at least one-fifth of the share capital, the members of the supervisory board should be elected at the meeting by voting in separate groups. This conclusion will also be effective if the articles of association provide for a different method of appointing the supervisory board. During the general meeting at which the members of the supervisory board are to be elected, voting will take place in separate groups of people representing the portion of the shares arising from the division. Within the group, the selection of the given supervisory board member candidate is determined by a resolution passed by a majority of votes and, if such a group elects one member of the supervisory board, the members of that group will not participate in the election of the other members of the supervisory board.[66]

346. However, the other posts are filled through voting in which all shareholders, whose votes have not been cast when electing members of the supervisory board through voting in separate groups, take part.

347. Additionally, in the case of group voting, each group only has one vote without preferences or restrictions.

348. The members of the supervisory board may be awarded a salary, which is specified in the articles of association.

349. The term of office of a member of the supervisory board may not be longer than five years.

66. Article 385 §5 CCCP.

350. The supervisory board constantly exercises control over the operation of the company. The supervisory board may examine all documents, request explanations from the management board and the employees and provide the balance of the company's assets. The supervisory board also passes resolutions approving certain activities of the management board.

351. It has the right to specify the status, for example, through the introduction of the requirement to obtain the consent of the supervisory board for the management board to perform specific activities.

352. The supervisory board performs its duties collectively. In principle, resolutions are passed at meetings, although, in some cases, they may also be passed electronically.

353. A very important right of the supervisory board is the ability to delegate its members to perform specific supervisory activities independently and, as will be discussed below, to delegate its members to the management board.

II. Administrative or Management Body

A. *Directors and Administrative Board (Appointment Requirements, Remuneration, Dismissal)*

354. The management board of a joint-stock company may consist of one or more people. The board members should be specified by the company's articles of association. A shareholder or a person from among the shareholders can be a member of the management board. Polish law does not allow commercial law companies to be members of the management board. Only a natural person with full legal capacity may be a member of the management board of a joint-stock company.

B. *Powers of Management and Representation*

355. A member of the management board has the right to both represent the company and manage its affairs. It is presumed under Polish law that the members of the management board have the right to handle the company's affairs. In particular, the general meeting (owner) of the company does not have the right to give binding instructions on the management of the company's affairs. It should simultaneously be mentioned that work is currently underway to amend the regulations so as to allow shareholders to have a more direct influence on the management of the company's affairs and decisions made by the company's governing bodies. This is because it is accepted that the prohibition of the general meeting to issue binding instructions on the management of the company's affairs to the management board is a legal fiction, which is frequently not observed. For example, the business press mentions certain State Treasury companies where informal pressure is applied on the members of the management board by the dominant shareholder. Decisions made by certain management boards in certain companies controlled by the State Treasury also give rise to reasonable doubts as to the economic sense. Therefore, it was rightly assumed in the legal literature that it would be healthier for such a right of a shareholder to influence the course of the company's affairs to be simply enshrined in the regulations.

356. The management board works collectively.[67]

357. A member of the management board may not be restricted in the representation of the company. This applies to all companies. However, it is possible to introduce a rule that a member of the management board will not be able to make decisions on his own or sign contracts on behalf of the company, but will have to act together with one or more members of the management board.

C. *Duties of Directors to the Company (Conflict of Interest) the Shareholders and Third Parties*

358. A member of the management board cannot take up competitive activities, participate in a competitive company as a partner in a civil partnership, or professional partnership or as a member of a governing body of a company or a legal person, as a member of the management board and may not participate in another company as the owner of at least 10% of the shares, or as a person authorized to appoint at least one member of the board without the company's consent.[68]

D. *Liability of Directors*

359. If a member of the management board breaches such a prohibition, he exposes himself to liability for damages to the company. The permission for a member of the management board to take up competitive activities is granted by the body authorized to appoint the management board; this will most frequently be the supervisory board or general meeting.

360. In addition, a member of the management board bears civil liability to the company for breaching the standard of conduct specified in the regulations; the CCCP also includes criminal sanctions in the case of particularly reprehensible actions of the members of the management board.

III. Auditor (Appointment, Powers, Duties)

361. The appointment of an auditor requires a decision of the respective authorities of the company.

67. Article 371 §1 CCCP.
68. Article 380 §1 CCCP.

IV. Workers' Participation (E.g., Via Two-Tier Board Structure or Auditor Appointment)

362. Poland has a long history of worker participation in the management of enterprises. Far-reaching rights were granted to the workers' council as early as in the 1980s, on the wave of moving away from the rigid dogmas of the centrally planned socialist economy. The workers' council had extensive participative rights in managing the enterprise. The award to employees of the right to participate in the management of the enterprise was a poor substitute for democracy in times when free elections were not held in Poland.[69]

363. However, free market reforms according to the classic free market model in its pure form from the 1990s ruled out the involvement of workers in the management of enterprises. This was considered a relic of the socialist times. The Polish provisions on commercial law do not contain requirements for the obligatory inclusion of workers in the governing bodies of companies. Such requirements may arise from specific regulations, e.g., the representatives of the employee are entitled to participate in the work of the supervisory board in joint-stock companies as the legal successors of the previously operating state-owned enterprises.

§6. Liquidation of the Corporation/Company

I. Grounds for Winding-Up (Court Decision, Shareholders' Meeting)

364. The liquidation of a joint-stock company is opened upon one of the following premises being satisfied:

(1) the premise provided for in the articles of association is manifested;
(2) a resolution is passed by the general meeting on the liquidation of the company or the transfer of the company's seat abroad;
(3) the company's bankruptcy is declared;
(4) an appropriate decision of the registration court is made.

II. The Effect of Winding-Up: Liquidation

365. The effect of opening liquidation is the need to liquidate the company. Liquidation is conducted by liquidators, who can only be natural persons. In principle, liquidators are members of the company's management board, unless otherwise arises from the articles of association or a court decision or an administrative decision.

69. Cf. S. Szmitka, *Specyfika cech prywatyzacji polskiej gospodarki początkowego okresu reform*, p. 85.

366. Liquidators are required to announce the dissolution of the company and the opening of its liquidation. They prepare the opening balance sheet of the liquidation. Then they perform liquidation activities, involving, in particular, ending the company's current receivables, collecting debts and receivables from shareholders, disposing of the assets and satisfying liabilities. Satisfying the interest of a creditor is one of the main objectives of the liquidation procedure.

367. The liquidation procedure ends with the liquidator preparing the financial statements as at the day preceding the distribution of the assets remaining after satisfying or securing the creditors among the shareholders. This is the so-called winding-up report. After preparing this report, the liquidators should call a general meeting to approve the report, announce it and submit the report to the registry court, while submitting a request to delete the company from the register.

368. The company is finally removed from the register after it has been wound up when the court makes its decision. The dissolved company's ledgers and documents should be kept for safekeeping by the person specified in the articles of association or in the resolution of the general meeting. And if there is no such indication, the registration court nominates the person who will store them.

§7. Mergers and Takeovers

I. Restrictions on Mergers & Takeovers

369. Polish law allows for an extensive range of mergers, namely equity, asset and organizational consolidation. Under Polish commercial law, mergers take place through universal succession, which eliminates the need for separate legal activities transferring individual one company's assets to another company.

370. The CCCP provides for two classic models of mergers. The first is merger by acquisition. The second is merger by establishing a new company.

371. Merger by acquisition involves the transfer of all assets of the company being acquired to the acquiring company in exchange for shares or stocks that the acquiring company issues to the shareholders of the company being acquired.

372. However, merging by establishing a new company involves establishing a company (namely a joint-stock company or a limited liability company), into which the assets of all merging companies are transferred in exchange for shares or stocks in the new company.

373. Both the acquiring company and the new company that is established under Polish law can only be a limited company, namely a limited liability company or joint-stock company.

374. All the assets of the company being acquired or the merging companies are transferred to the acquiring company or the companies that are merging through the establishment of a new company. However, the shareholders of these companies receive shares or stocks in the acquiring company or a new company in return for these assets.

375. The date of the merger will be the date on which legal effects related to the merger arise, namely the date of entry of the merger into the register of entrepreneurs.

376. A key element of the merger plan is the share exchange ratio. The CCCP itself does not introduce any restrictions on the methods of valuing the assets of companies that are being merged, but it should be remembered that both the correctness and reliability of the exchange parity established on the basis of the method used will be examined by experts appointed by a court.

377. The regulations on the establishment of the acquiring company or the newly established company that is formed as a result of the merger[70] are applied accordingly to company mergers.

378. The company being acquired or the companies that are merging through the formation of a new company are dissolved without liquidation on the date of deletion from the register (namely when a new company is entered into the register or the acquisition is registered).

379. General legal succession, namely the so-called universal succession arises at the time of the merger. The acquiring company or the newly established company takes over the permits, concessions and relief awarded to the acquired company or any of the companies which are merging through the establishment of the new company on the date of the merger unless a legal act or the decision to award the permit, concession or relief provide otherwise.

380. However, Polish law provides that the assets of each of the merged companies should be managed separately for a specified period after the merger. This should be done until the date on which the creditors, whose claims arose before the date of the merger and who demanded payment in writing within six months of the announcement of the merger, are satisfied or secured.

381. Merger proceedings essentially consist of three stages. Preparatory activities, the passage of a resolution on the merger, as well as registration and announcement of the merger. Polish regulations contain detailed rules on what each of these three stages looks like in the case of mergers of limited liability companies, as well as mergers of partnerships and mergers of partnerships with companies.

70. Article 497 §1 CCCP.

II. Dividing Corporations

382. Polish law also provides for the possibility of dividing companies, whereby only a limited liability company or a joint-stock company can be divided. It can be divided into two or more companies.[71] Therefore, partnerships cannot be divided.

383. Polish law provides for four types of division of companies. These are:

(1) division by acquisition, which involves the transfer of all assets of the company being divided to other companies in exchange for shares in the acquiring company, which are taken up by the shareholders of the company being divided;[72]
(2) division through the formation of new companies, which involves establishing new companies to which all the assets of the company being divided are transferred in exchange for shares in the new companies;[73]
(3) division by acquisition and the establishment of a new company. This method involves the transfer of all assets of the company being divided to an existing company and the reestablishment of the company or companies;[74]
(4) division by separation, involving the transfer of part of the assets of the company being divided to an existing or newly incorporated company or companies for shares of the acquiring company or companies, newly incorporated companies or the divided company, which are taken up by the shareholders of the divided company;[75]
(5) division by spin-off. The method consists of transferring part of the assets of the company being divided to an existing or newly incorporated company or companies for the shares of the acquiring or newly incorporated company or companies that the divided company includes.[76]

384. The CCCP contains detailed rules for each of these types of divisions. Proceedings on the division of companies, just like mergers of companies, are divided into three stages—preparatory activities, the passage of a resolution on the division, and the registration of the announcement of the division.

III. Protective Measures

385. Capital market control mechanisms, such as hostile takeovers, have a negligible role in the Polish economy. The Polish capital market is not developed. The stock exchange plays practically no role in the valuation and control of Polish enterprises, while its role as a mechanism for allocating financial capital is very small.

71. Article 528 §1 CCCP. From Aug. 16, 2023, the limited joint-stock partnership is also subject to division.
72. Article 529 §1, item 1 CCCP.
73. Article 529 §1, item 2 CCCP.
74. Article 529 §1, item 3 CCCP.
75. Article 529 §1, item 4 CCCP.
76. Article 529 §1, item 5 CCCP.

The main factor determining this is the operation of Polish joint-stock companies under a closed system of corporate governance. The concentration of rights to shares in the hands of strategic investors, who are therefore able to control the activities of managers is typical of a closed system of corporate governance. Poland has a high level of concentration of rights to share in the hands of strategic shareholders of companies. Additionally, the existence and frequent application of preference shares and cross-shareholding relations between companies reinforces these phenomena.[77]

§8. Holding Companies and Subsidiaries

386. The same rules as described for limited liability companies apply. Please *see* the relevant points.

§9. Taxation of Corporations and Shareholders

387. A joint-stock company is not a taxpayer of corporate income tax (CIT). CIT is regulated in the Act on Corporate Income Tax of 1992. This is a tax collected on income. In the Polish legal system, CIT is income to the state budget. A proportion of the income from CIT from taxpayers with their registered offices in a given municipality goes to the municipality (6.71%). Additionally, 1.40% of the income from CIT of legal persons established in a former county goes to that county. Additionally, 14.75% of the income from CIT from taxpayers with their registered offices in a given voivodship goes to that voivodship. In other words, 80% of the total amount of CIT remains in the state budget, while over 20% of CIT goes to the budgets of local government units.

388. Legal persons and limited companies in formation are taxpayers of CIT. Unincorporated entities with their registered offices or management boards in another country are also taxpayers of this tax if, in accordance with the provisions of the tax laws of that other country, they are treated as legal persons and are taxable in that state on the whole of their income regardless of the place where it is generated.[78]

389. Tax groups, namely groups of at least two incorporated commercial law companies (namely limited liability companies or joint-stock companies) that are related through equity may also be taxpayers.[79]

---

77. Cf. A. Koch & J. Napierała, *Prawo* ..., p. 454 and P. Tamowicz & M. Dzierżanowski, *Własność i kontrola polskich korporacji* [eng. *Ownership and Control of Polish Corporations*], Gdańsk 2001, p. 7.
78. Cf. R. Oktaba, *Prawo podatkowe* [eng. *Tax Law*], Warsaw 2019, p. 253.
79. Cf. J. Marciniuk, editorial board, *Podatek dochodowy od osób prawnych. Komentarz* [eng. *Corporate Income Tax. Commentary*], Warsaw 2011, p. 14.

390. In tax terms, a group can become an individual taxpayer if it satisfies a number of conditions. They are as follows:

(1) the entities forming the tax group can only be limited liability companies, simple joint-stock companies or joint-stock companies with their registered offices in Poland if the average share capital attributable to each of these companies is no less than PLN 500,000;
(2) the parent company in the tax group directly holds a 75% share of the share capital of other companies;
(3) the subsidiaries do not hold a share of the share capital of other companies forming that group;
(4) the subsidiaries do not have any arrears in the payment of taxes constituting income to the state budget;
(5) the parent company and the subsidiaries have concluded an agreement in the form of a notarial deed on the establishment of a tax group for a period of at least three years and this agreement has been registered by the head of the tax office (the agreement should specify both the list of companies forming the tax group, the specification of the term of the agreement and a specification of the accepted tax year);
(6) the companies forming the tax group do not benefit from income tax exemptions under separate laws after this group is established;
(7) the tax group generates a share of revenue of at least 2% in every tax year.[80]

391. After registering the agreement on the tax group, it may not be increased with other companies or reduced by any of the companies forming this group, with the exception of the acquisition of a company initially forming the tax group by other companies from that group. The parent company, namely the company representing the tax group, will calculate the collection and remittance of income tax and advances on that tax. The companies forming the tax group are jointly and severally liable for their income tax liabilities that are due throughout the term of the agreement.

392. The aggregate income generated, capital gains and income obtained from other sources of revenue are taxable with CIT. Revenue will be taxable in certain cases. Income from the sources of revenue should be understood as the surplus of total revenues obtained from that source of revenue over the costs of generating that revenue, which is achieved in the tax year.

393. In CIT, the tax base is the income obtained from the difference between revenues and the costs of generating those revenues in a given tax year, after making any possible deductions.

394. The CIT rate in Poland is 19% of the tax base. In the case of taxation of small taxpayers, the initial rate is 9% of the tax base (since 2019) of the possible deductions.

80. Article 1a, paras. 1 and 2 of the Act on CIT.

395. The CIT rate in Poland is 19% of the tax base. In the case of taxation of so-called small taxpayers (these are taxpayers with a value of sales revenues of no more than the equivalent of EUR 2,000,000 in the previous tax year) the tax rate is 9% of the tax base (since 2019), with the reservation that these regulations do not apply in the tax year in which the small taxpayer started operating and in the tax year immediately after that year.

396. If taxpayers, who have their registered office in Poland, also generate revenues outside Poland and this income is taxed in the foreign country, when settling income for the tax year, this income is combined with income generated in Poland. However, an amount equal to the tax paid in the foreign country is deducted from the tax calculated on the aggregated income.

397. The tax rate on income from dividends and other income from a share of profits of legal persons who have their registered office or management board in Poland is 19%.

398. The act includes exemptions for both entities (e.g., State Treasury) and activities. The most important exemptions on activities include a CIT exemption on the sale of all or a part of the real property constituting a part of a farm.

399. Taxpayers of CIT are required to calculate the monthly tax advances at the amount of the difference between the tax due on income from the beginning of the tax year and the sum of the advance payments due for prior months.

400. Taxpayers pay monthly advances by the twentieth day of each month for the previous month. The taxpayer pays the advance for the last month of the tax year by the twentieth day of the first month of the following tax year. Advances may also be paid quarterly.

401. In addition, all legal persons, unincorporated organizational units and sole proprietors are remitters of Value Added Tax (VAT).

402. A joint-stock company is also a remitter of VAT. Additionally, if a joint-stock company has the status of a public benefit organization, organizational units of that company may be remitters, provided that they conduct business activities and independently prepare financial statements. The status of a public benefit organization may be granted to a joint-stock company (and a limited liability company), which:

- does not operate to generate a profit;
- allocates the whole of its income to the achievement of its statutory objectives;
- does not distribute profit for distribution to its shareholders, stockholders or employees.

Chapter 2. Simple Joint-Stock Company

§1. Origin of the Regulation

403. The PSA was introduced into Polish law by an amendment to the CCCP of July 2019. This amendment is the biggest amendment to the Code since its adoption. The regulations entered into force on July 1, 2021.

404. By assumption, a PSA is supposed to be a modern type of closed company and an alternative to a limited liability company as the basic form of doing business for a limited group of investors.

405. Work on the regulations for a PSA started in 2016. Various concepts were considered. One of them assumed that the regulations on the limited liability company would be modified. However, it was acknowledged that the reform of the regulations on limited liability companies would in fact mean that most of these provisions would need to be adopted almost from the beginning. There were also concerns about the disruption of the operation of almost 500,000 existing limited liability companies in Poland.

406. However, in order to introduce a model of a simple company, such as a limited liability company, this would mean that many variants would need to be introduced, which would complicate the regulations of the CCCP.

407. Consequently, it was accepted that the best solution would be to establish a new legal form of a company, which is independent of these types of capital companies to date. The provisions on a PSA require the application of the regulations of other types of companies to a PSA only where this was not necessary for preparing separate regulations.

§2. Scope of Regulations

408. The regulation that was introduced actually competes simultaneously with the existing regulations. The decision to choose the PSA as the legal model for an investment vehicle rests with the founders. They are still able to use the classic model of a joint-stock company and the model of a limited liability company.

§3. Foreign Inspiration

409. It should also be mentioned that the decision of the Polish lawmakers is in line with the direction of reform of the company law regulations in many other countries. Several other European countries have also introduced a PSA, alongside the existing legal forms of capital companies—these will be France, Luxembourg and Slovakia. However, some countries have implemented a thorough reform of the existing legal forms of companies, such as the Netherlands and Belgium.

§4. CHARACTERISTICS

410. A PSA differs from a limited liability company primarily in terms of the freedom to form the company's political system and model of membership in the company.[81]

411. According to the assumptions of the developers, a PSA is expected to be adapted to perform various roles. Therefore, it should enable both start-ups and larger joint ventures, as well as companies used for one-off transactions (SPVs) to operate.

412. While discussing the most important features of a PSA with respect to the previous types of commercial companies under Polish law, the actual developer of this regulation, Prof. A., Opalski mentions five elements.

413. First of all, the shareholders of simple joint-stock companies received the ability to contribute work and services in exchange for the shares to which they subscribed. In this respect, the solutions in the PSA differ from the rules in force in ordinary joint-stock companies and in a limited liability company. It also means that the institution of share capital was abandoned in a PSA. The developers of this regulation mention that this solution satisfies the needs of start-up type enterprises, which combine the innovative skills, knowledge and concepts of the founders with capital which is provided by the investors by enabling the contribution of work and services in exchange for taking up shares which was admitted as a method of paying for participation in a PSA in the same way as the classic method of making capital contributions.

414. Second, assets corresponding to the value of the capital contributions made to the company may be returned to the shareholders if it is not needed to finance the business and does not pose a threat to the interests of the company's creditors. Common stock of a PSA was introduced into the concept, constituting share capital, which is one of the acceptable sources of payment of a dividend, payment for redeeming shares and payment of the price for the acquisition by the company of its own shares. The shares of a PSA do not have a nominal value. In the justification, it is indicated that a fixed amount of share capital is most frequently not adapted to the needs of the company and its creditors while blocking capital transfers and hindering restructuring.

415. Third, the shareholders of a PSA can largely determine the mutual relations and form the system of membership rights. Therefore, further reaching share preferences are possible than in an ordinary joint-stock company.

416. Fourth, the shares of a PSA are permanently dematerialized and disclosed in the register kept by public trust entities.

---

81. Cf. A. Opalski, *Prosta Spółka Akcyjna: nowy typ spółki handlowej (część I)* [eng. *Simple Joint Stock Company: A New Type of Commercial Company (Part I)*], PPH 2019, No. 11.

417. Fifth, the founders of a PSA have received a choice between classic structures of company management with management boards and a supervisory board and a model of a board of directors based on the Anglo-American models. This should increase the attractiveness of this legal form for foreign investors who are accustomed to this model in their own countries. Simultaneously, the rules on civil liability have been modernized, providing the members of the board of directors with a release from liability in the event of action within the limits of reasonable economic risk.

§5. Rights of the Shareholders

418. Shareholders have extensive autonomy in determining mutual relations and forming membership rights. As mentioned above when discussing the regulations on the limited liability company and joint-stock company, preference in voting and preference of the dividend in ordinary forms of limited liability companies are limited. The preference in voting can exceed three votes per share, while the preference in the case of the dividend can exceed more than half the dividend that is attributable to the remaining shares.

419. In a PSA, it has been accepted that the restrictions on preferences that may be granted to individual stockholders or shareholders are unjustified. The ability to structure the internal relations between the shareholders of a PSA as they deem fit should not be restricted by rigid and arbitrary criteria. Therefore, in the provisions on the PSA, there are no rigid restrictions on the preferences attached to shares and individual rights granted to the shareholders.[82] The list of preferences and permissions is not exhaustive. Non-voting shares may also be issued. They should be preference shares in terms of dividends.

§6. Asset Situation in a PSA

420. An in-kind contribution to a PSA made in exchange for shares that are acquired may be any contribution of material value, in particular work or services.[83]

421. It transpires from the above regulation that there are two categories of contributions in a PSA. Each of these categories is subject to a separate legal regime. There is a classic contribution, namely capital contributions—contributions in cash and in-kind that have the capability of being contributions in kind in other companies, such as real estate, as well as any other contributions, which could not be made as a contribution in other companies. In the first place, this will be work and services.

82. Article 300^{25} CCCP and Art. 300^{28} §1 CCCP.
83. Article 300^{2} §2 CCCP.

422. The declared contributions in relations between shareholders and therefore in internal relations are essentially valued by the shareholders using any method. There is no obligation to cover the nominal value of the shares; this nominal value does not exist in a PSA. The valuation of contributions will be reflected in the number of shares allocated to the shareholders. In other words, the number of shares allocated to the shareholders in exchange for specific contributions will arise from a decision made by the shareholders, and not from an objective value of the contribution, which is verifiable by third parties. According to some representatives of the Polish legal doctrine, the freedom of valuation of contributions does not create a threat to the company's participants.[84] This author indicates that noncapital contributions can often play a key role in the company's ability to generate revenue. This will be the case, for example, if an outstanding specialist in technology undertakes to provide his experience in work. However, it is difficult to establish the objectively verifiable value of such a person's work. Issuing shares in exchange for work therefore expresses a certain anticipation of the success of the joint venture.

423. Share capital in a PSA consists of capital contributions, made to the company and obligatory write-downs to profit. Payments to shareholders and write-downs intended to cover the company's losses have been reduced. Interestingly, in a PSA, the amount of share capital is not an element of the founding agreement between the company's shareholders and is not specified in the articles of association. It is the result of arrangements regarding the capital contributions to be made to the company, as well as their timing and the effects of the management of the company's funds by shareholders. Therefore, it is only when the contribution is actually made that the amount of the share capital increases. The level of share capital does not change as a result of a change in the articles of association (as in all other companies), but only as a result of new contributions being made as a result of shares being issued, or some of the funds being disbursed from the share capital to the shareholders. Therefore, the share capital differs from the share capital in an ordinary joint-stock company and in a limited liability company. Share capital in a PSA is variable; it varies according to events. The management board is responsible for reporting the amount of share capital to the register and keeping it constantly updated.[85]

424. The shares in a PSA have no nominal value. They do not constitute a fraction of the share capital. There is no minimum value of contribution in a PSA which has to be made to pay for the shares. This makes it easier to contribute the service of work as a contribution.

425. Shareholders in a PSA not only have the right to a share of the profit but also the right to make withdrawals from the share capital. Therefore, it is possible to withdraw equity funds from the company in a PSA.[86]

---

84. Cf. A. Opalski, *Prosta Spółka Akcyjna: nowy typ spółki handlowej (część I)*, PPH 2019, No. 11, p. 9.
85. Article 300^{12} §2, item 6 CCCP and Art. 300^{104} §2 CCCP.
86. Article 300^{15} §1 CCCP.

426. As can be seen from the above, the principles of the property regime in a PSA are far more flexible and beneficial for shareholders than in an ordinary joint-stock company or a limited liability company. Therefore, this had to be balanced by appropriate protective instruments for the company's creditors. Several elements have been introduced in this respect.

427. First of all, the obligation has been introduced to provide share capital with write-downs to profit to cover the company's future losses.[87]

428. Second, additional rules were introduced regarding the return of some of the accumulated equity funds to shareholders. In this case, the rule applies that withdrawals may be freely made from share capital up to 50% of the sum of the company's liabilities arising from the approved financial statements for the last financial year.

429. Third, there is also a prohibition on making payments to shareholders that would pose a threat to the company's solvency.[88]

§7. Organization Structure in a PSA

430. The key rule regarding the operation of simple joint-stock companies is set out in Article 300^{53} of the CCCP. According to this rule, members of the management board and directors of a PSA are subject to the restrictions arising from the resolutions of the shareholders. The managers of companies are therefore required to comply with those resolutions of the shareholders, which impose a specific course of action on them. Such resolutions can contain binding instructions or other restrictions on the method of managing the company's affairs. It was acknowledged in this way that the shareholders, as the economic owners of the company, constitute its highest governing body, which has the power to intervene in the management of the company, regardless of whether the articles of association attach any explicit authorization to this or not. It should be noted that the general meeting is prohibited from giving orders to the management board in an ordinary joint-stock company. This rule does not apply in a PSA.

431. An option has been introduced into a PSA of choosing a management structure according to one of the three input models of the company's executive bodies. The first model is the appointment of the management board as the sole executive body. The second is the appointment of a management board and a supervisory board, while the third model is the appointment of a board of directors.[89]

87. Article 300^{19} CCCP.
88. Article 300^{15} §5 CCCP.
89. Article 300^{52} CCCP.

432. The simplest model is obviously the model with just the management board. Such a model is used in the vast majority of limited liability companies operating in Poland.

433. In turn, the model of the management board and supervisory board is the model used in the case of a joint-stock company in which a supervisory board must be appointed. If the shareholders decide to choose this model in a PSA, the supervisory board will have the power to appoint and remove the members of the management board. An interesting novelty—compared to the existing regulation of an ordinary joint-stock company—is the award to the supervisory board of the independent right to specify the activities that the management board can perform only after obtaining the consent of the supervisory board (second sentence of Article 300^{69} §4 of the CCCP).

434. In turn, the third model, namely the ability to appoint a board of directors, is innovative under Polish law. Simultaneously, by appointing a board of directors, the shareholders are able to adapt their model to the individual needs of the enterprise. A board of directors consisting of only one person can simultaneously be appointed, although, of course, the appointment of a board of directors with more than one person will be the norm. The board of directors can delegate the performance of the company's business activities to some of the directors who have the status of executive directors at that time, while others become nonexecutive directors and exercise ongoing supervision of the company's affairs.[90]

435. The board of directors then has functions of handling the company's affairs, as well as representation and supervision. In the case of a division into executive and nonexecutive directors, each of these functions is performed by a different category of directors.

436. The boundaries for the autonomy of the parties are specified by three principles. First of all, the most important decisions specified in the Act require the collegial decision of all directors.[91] These include decision-making of strategic significance to the company or determining the business plans and the organizational structure of the company's business. Second, the delegation may only encompass activities of running the company's business, while all corporate activities, such as calling general meetings, are the responsibility of the board of directors. Third, all directors have the nontransferrable and unlimited power to represent the company.[92]

437. On the one hand, the rules on the liability of the board members with respect to joint-stock companies and limited liability companies are relaxed, but on the other hand, they modify rules that have been criticized as being inconsistent and

---

90. Article 300^{76} §1 CCCP.
91. Article 300^{75} §2 and §3 CCCP.
92. Article 300^{77} CCCP. Cf. A. Opalski, *Prosta Spółka Akcyjna: nowy typ spółki handlowej (część I)*, PPH 2019, No. 11, p. 8.

insufficiently protecting companies in the case of ordinary companies. The basis of civil liability of the members of the governing bodies of a PSA to the company is their failure to exercise due diligence while performing their function if this is at fault. Therefore, there is no need to prove the lawlessness of a specific action of a member of the governing body by indicating a particular provision of the law or of the articles of association that has been breached. However, if a member of the body acts within the limits of reasonable economic risk, he is released from liability.[93] This rule does not apply to ordinary joint-stock companies or limited liability companies. This is a correct rule enabling the company's managers to accept a slightly higher risk.

§8. Form of Shares

438. The shares of a PSA only appear in dematerialized form.[94] It is prohibited to issue shares in the form of documents. The shares of a PSA are disclosed in the register of shareholders kept by entities of public trust.

439. On the sideline, it should be pointed out that, in the near future, shares in all joint-stock companies and limited joint-stock partnerships will necessarily have to be dematerialized because of the amendment to the respective provisions of the CCCP.

440. The principles of dematerialization of the shares in a PSA are consistent with the new regime for the dematerialization of shares, which is being introduced into the provisions on an ordinary joint-stock company.

441. The register of shareholders may only be kept in electronic form.[95]

§9. Liquidation

442. A PSA can be liquidated more simply than an ordinary joint-stock company. The regulations allow for the possibility of terminating the company's existence (removing it from the register of entrepreneurs) without conducting liquidation proceedings if the company's assets are acquired by one of the shareholders with the obligation to satisfy the creditors and other shareholders.[96] The company's assets are acquired by the acquiring shareholder on the basis of a resolution of the general meeting passed by a qualified majority of three-quarters of the votes provided that shareholders representing at least half of the total number of shares take part in the voting.

93. Article 300^{125} §2 CCCP.
94. Article 300^{29}, §1 CCCP.
95. Article 300^{31} §3 CCCP.
96. Article 300^{122} CCCP.

§10. Taxation (In Brief)

443. A PSA is a taxpayer of CIT. More on this subject in the part about taxation in an ordinary joint-stock company.

444. A PSA is also a remitter of VAT. Additionally, if a PSA has the status of a public benefit organization, organizational units of that company may be remitters, provided that they conduct business activities and independently prepare financial statements.

§11. Conclusion

445. In concluding the presentation of the regulations regarding the PSA, it should be pointed out that the introduction of this regulation has encountered mass criticism in Polish legal doctrine. A large proportion of academics dealing with commercial law claim that a PSA poses a threat to the security of trading and creditors of these companies because their structure allows companies to operate without assets. Second, it was accepted that this company posed a threat to investors because no preference limits had been set for the shares. Third, the solutions provided for in the structure of a PSA are not harmonized with the system of company law and breach its consistency.

Chapter 3. Company Transformations

§1. Origin of the Regulations and Current Status

446. The comprehensive regulation of the transformation of companies, which was implemented in 2000, was a novelty in Polish law. Earlier regulations only allowed for the transformation of a joint-stock company into a limited liability company and a limited liability company into a joint-stock company.

447. The current regulation has significantly increased the subjective scope of entities that may be subject to transformation. The change in the legal form of companies is currently acceptable to a large extent. A partnership may be transformed into a company, a company into a partnership, a company into another type of company and a partnership into another type of partnership.

448. The general principle in Polish law is that any company or partnership can be transformed into any other company or partnership. The simplest partnership, a general partnership, can be transformed into the most extensive form of company—a joint-stock company.

449. The provisions of the CCCP, allowing the transformation of commercial law companies in virtually any manner, also apply to a civil partnership, although a civil partnership, as mentioned above, is not a separate legal form, but purely an agreement. A civil partnership can now be converted into another company.

§2. Essence of the Transformation

450. The essence of the transformation of the company involves changing the legal form of the company. The transformed company is entitled to all the rights and duties of the company being transformed. There is no legal succession in the transformation, unlike in the case of mergers or divisions of companies. The transformed company does not accede to any rights and obligations of the transformed company, but these are its own rights and obligations. The company remains the same, only its legal form changes. Therefore, the previously acquired rights and obligations are vested in it in whole and without any changes. This means that the transformed company remains the holder of the permits, concessions and relief granted before the transformation. There may be exceptions in this respect, however, arising from special provisions other than the provisions of commercial law. For example, a bank can only be run in the form of a joint-stock company, so transforming a joint-stock company into another commercial law company would mean losing its banking license.

451. In principle, the transformation does not change the membership of the partners. As at the date of transformation, the partners of the company being transformed who participate in the transformation become partners of the transformed company.

452. The transformed company should also use the former name in brackets for at least a year from the date of transformation. This is only not an obligation if the change in the wording of the company's name in connection with the transformation only involves changing the additional name indicating the nature of the company.

§3. General Rules Regarding the Transformation of Companies and the Effects of the Transformation

453. The general rule regarding the method of transformation itself is that the transformation of the company should be subject to the appropriate regulations regarding the establishment of the transformed company.

454. As a rule, the transformation of the company requires (unless otherwise stated in the regulations on the transformation of certain types of companies, as referred to below):

- the preparation of a transformation plan of the company together with an auditor's opinion;
- the passage of a resolution on the company's transformation;
- the appointment of members of the governing bodies of the transformed company or the specification of the partner representing the partnership and managing its affairs;
- the conclusion of the articles or the signature of the transformed company's statutes;
- the entry of the transformed company into the register and the deletion of the transformed company.

455. The transformation plan is prepared by the management board of the transformed company or by all partners handling the affairs of the transformed partnership. In the case of companies, this will therefore be the company's management board (the company's management board will also be required to prepare a transformation plan in the partner company the management board of which has been established). In partnerships, the obligation to prepare a transformation plan rests with the partners managing the partnership's affairs. The transformation plan should be prepared in writing otherwise null and void, whereas, in the case of a sole proprietorship, it should be prepared in the form of a notarial deed.

456. The transformation plan should contain at least the establishment of the book value of the transformed company's assets as at a specific day in the month preceding the presentation of the transformation plan to the shareholders and the determination of the value of the shareholders' shares or stocks in accordance with the financial statements prepared for transformation purposes.

457. A number of documents should be attached to the transformation plan. These are:

- A draft resolution on the transformation of the company.
- The draft articles or the statutes of the transformed company.
- The valuation of the transformed company's assets.
- The financial statements prepared for the purpose of transformation.

458. The transformation plan needs to be audited for correctness and reliability and in order to establish whether the evaluation of the assets and liabilities of the company under transformation is reliable.[97] The transformation plan is audited by a statutory auditor.

459. The resolution on the transformation is passed in the case of partnerships by the partners and in the case of companies by the shareholders' meeting or general meeting. The resolution should specify, among others:[98]

- the legal form of company into which the company is being transformed;
- the amount of share capital in the case of transformation into a company or the capital account in the case of transformation into a limited partnership;
- the rights granted personally to the shareholders or partners taking part in the transformed company or partnership if such rights are to be granted;
- the surnames and forenames of the members of the management board of the transformed company in the case of transformation into a company, or the surnames and forenames of the partners handling the partnership's affairs having to represent the transformed partnership in the case of transformation into a partnership;
- approval of the transformation plan, as well as the proposed wording of the articles or the statutes of the transformed company or partnership.

460. The transformation itself is then entered in the register. The application for the entry of the transformation into the register will be filed by all members of the management board or partners authorized to represent the transformed partnership.

461. The mere fact of the transformation is then announced at the request of the management board of the transformed company or all partners handling the affairs of the transformed partnership.

462. As a result of the transformation, the shareholders/partners of the company/partnership being transformed become partners/shareholders of the transformed partnership/company.[99]

463. Until recently, the rule under Polish law was that each shareholder decides independently whether he wants to participate in the transformation. Shareholders who did not want to participate in the transformation had to be paid off. Such shareholders had the right to demand payment of an amount corresponding to the value

97. Article 559 §1 CCCP.
98. Article 563 CCCP.
99. Article 553 §3 CCCP.

of their shares in the transformed company. This value was established on the basis of specially prepared financial statements of the shareholders who did not assume a share of the transformed company.

464. It was argued in the Polish legal doctrine that the rule ordering shareholders not taking part in the transformation to be paid off in each case and without any additional restrictions actually prevented the transformation from being made in many cases. These provisions were amended for this reason when making amendments to the CCCP regarding the PSA. The most important change is the waiver of the principle of presumption of a lack of participation in the transformed company by the shareholders or stockholders of the company being transformed. Simultaneously, the new institution of "exit rights" was introduced, which involves demanding the right to demand the buyback of the shares in the transformed company.[100] However, this right only applies to the transformation of a company (limited liability company or joint-stock company) into a partnership, and only to a partner who voted against the resolution on the transformation and demanded that the objection be entered into the minutes.

465. The correctness of the passage of the transformation resolution may also be questioned by partners/shareholders on the basis of the general rules regarding appealing against resolutions of the company authorities.

466. People representing a transformed company are jointly and severally liable to the company, partners/shareholders and third parties for damage caused by acts or omissions which are in conflict with the law or the provisions of the articles of association or the statutes unless they are not at fault.

§4. Special Rules for Transforming Particular Types of Companies

467. In addition, the CCCP provides for specific rules regarding the transformation of individual types of companies into other companies. Therefore, for instance, special rules apply to the principles on which a partnership is transformed into a company with regard to the share requirements, the method in which resolutions are passed and similar matters.

468. In some cases, these special rules also involve relaxing the requirements with respect to those mentioned above. For example, no plan is prepared in the case of the transformation of a general partnership, in which all partners handled the partnership's affairs, into a limited company or another partnership.

469. In the case of the transformation of a company into another company, the lawmakers introduced special rules regarding even such matters as the obligation to

100. Article 576 §1 CCCP.

cover the share capital of the joint-stock company being transformed, the minimum amount of share capital of the transformed company or the method in which the transformation resolution is passed.

Chapter 4. Closed Corporation: Private Company—Limited Liability Company

§1. CHARACTERISTICS

470. A limited liability company is the most popular legal form among all commercial companies in Poland. It is sufficient to mention that over 450,000 limited liability companies are operating in Poland, while there are slightly more than 10,000 joint-stock companies.

471. The popularity of a limited liability company in Poland stems from two main factors.

472. First of all, a limited liability company is a relatively uncomplicated form of company; the procedure for establishing and subsequently operating the company is quite simple.

473. Second, the shareholders are not personally liable for the company's liabilities.

474. The structure of a limited liability company in Polish law has many features in common with the model adopted in Germany. Both the solutions adopted in the Prewar Commercial Code and the solutions adopted in the current CCCP demonstrate that the authors of these provisions were clearly inspired by the German solutions.

475. A limited liability company is one of two forms of company. Shareholders have greater rights than in the case of a joint-stock company, but the management model is based on governing bodies, the members of which may be the shareholders, although they are frequently people from outside the group of shareholders.

476. Limited liability companies are used to run very small businesses, as well as multibillion-zloty enterprises.

477. However, limited liability companies cannot be listed on the Warsaw Stock Exchange, so if these entities are thinking about flotation on the stock exchange, they need to be transformed into a joint-stock company.

478. A limited liability company contains both purely equity elements as well as personal elements. The equity elements are primarily the limitation of the liability of the company's shareholders for the company's liabilities. The company itself is obviously liable to the creditors with all its assets; although the limitation of liability applies to the shareholders—the risk to their assets is limited to the company's assets. The shareholders are not liable at all for the company's liabilities.

479. Another equity element is the fact that the company operates on the basis of a fixed, predetermined share capital, which is specified in the articles of association.

480. The personnel membership of a limited liability company changes frequently; in practice, they do not require any requirements to be satisfied. The most typical reason for such a change is the disposal of shares in the company by a shareholder, which results in the transfer of these shares to another person. The buyer can either be one of the shareholders or third parties.

481. The sign of the equity nature of a limited liability company can also be the fact that sole proprietorships can and in fact do often operate.

482. In turn, the personal elements that are also found in a limited liability company are primarily the right to exercise personal control over the company's activities and operations by the individual shareholders. Shareholders in a joint-stock company do not have such rights.

483. A personal element in a limited liability company is also the fact that the court is able to exclude a shareholder or even dissolve a company.

484. The prohibition to issue bearer or registered or commissioned documents embodying shareholder rights is also considered a personal element in a limited liability company.

485. Likewise, the personal nature of this company is indicated by the fact that the articles of association can limit the accession to the company of the heirs of a deceased shareholder.

486. The final element suggesting at least the partially personal nature of a limited liability company is the ability of the meeting of shareholders to issue binding recommendations to the management board. In the case of a joint-stock company, general meetings cannot issue binding orders to the management board. However, it should be noted that, in 2020, work is in progress on the amendment of the CCCP. One of the issues that may be amended is precisely this prohibition to issue binding instructions to the management board by the general meeting of the joint-stock company.

§2. Formation

I. Formal Requirements (E.g., Notarial Record) and Minimum Content of Articles

487. The articles of association of a limited liability company may be concluded in one of two ways.

488. The main method is for the shareholders to conclude the articles of association in the form of a notarial deed and make an entry into the register of entrepreneurs on the basis of an application submitted to the National Court Register. In this model, the articles of a limited liability company must be in the form of a notarial deed.

489. The second, so-called accelerated mode is a model for establishing a limited liability company using a template of these articles. In this procedure of establishing a company, the forms need to be completed in an Information and Communication Technologies (ICTs) system, and the data should be sent in the ICT system to the register of entrepreneurs. The form of a notarial deed does not apply to this model. However, the completed form should have a qualified electronic signature or a trusted signature. The articles are considered concluded after entering all data necessary for their conclusion into the system and signing them with an electronic signature.[101]

490. The articles of association should contain the following provisions:

- the company's name and seat;
- the company's objects;
- the indication of the share capital; the number and nominal value of the shares subscribed to by the individual shareholders;
- a decision on whether a shareholder can hold more than one share;
- the term of the company, if defined;
- a detailed specification of the in-kind contribution and the name of the shareholder making such an in-kind contribution, the number and nominal value of shares acquired for this type of contribution;
- special benefits or duties if they are imposed on the shareholder in the articles of association.

491. In addition to the minimum components, the articles of association may include other elements that the shareholders can include in the articles essentially freely.

492. However, if a limited liability company is established in twenty-four-hour mode based on the template of the articles of the limited liability company provided in the IT system, the company's founders choose individual variants of the provisions from those that are available in the template made available in the IT system. The minimum elements listed above are the same and they must also be included in the articles of association using the ICT system.

---

101. Article 157 CCCP.

II. Notification, Registration, Incorporation and Publicity

493. A limited liability company is entered into the register of entrepreneurs, which is kept at the National Court Register and is only established when it is entered into this register. The register is publicly accessible. The register contains basic information on every entity registered there, including limited liability companies.

III. Contracts Made on Behalf of a Company in Formation

494. A so-called limited liability company in formation is established after the conclusion of the articles of association of a limited liability company, but before it is entered into the register. A limited liability company in formation is transformed into the appropriate limited liability company upon being entered into the register. A company in formation has legal personality, i.e., it can accept obligations and acquire rights on its own behalf. She can also sue and be sued. The company should use its trade name with the addition "in formation" in its activities. The company is represented by the management board or a proxy appointed by a resolution of the shareholders, while the company and the people acting on its behalf are jointly and severally liable for its liabilities, as is the shareholder, up to the value of the contribution made to cover the shares acquired. The liability of these last persons is limited until the approval of their activities by the shareholders' meeting after the company is established.[102]

495. In matters that are not regulated, the provisions on the appropriate limited liability company apply to a limited liability company in formation.

496. A limited liability company must be reported for registration in the register within six months of the date of conclusion of the articles. If the company is not reported to the register within this time, the articles of association are automatically dissolved. This deadline is much shorter for companies formed in the electronic procedure and is seven days. If the company itself is unable to perform these activities forthwith, liquidators are appointed and it is liquidated.

IV. Number of Shareholders

497. The law does not impose any restrictions on the minimum number of shareholders; one person is sufficient. However, as sole proprietorship that is a limited liability company cannot establish another limited liability company. However, this

102. Article 161 CCCP.

does not prevent the formation of such a structure after the limited liability company is established. Consequently, a limited liability company may be formed by two shareholders, including a sole proprietorship that is a limited liability company, and then the shares may be transferred from the other partner to that sole proprietor's limited liability company.

498. There is no maximum number of shareholders. There may be any number.

V. Initial Share Capital

499. The minimum share capital of a limited company is PLN 5,000, which is slightly more than EUR 1,000.

VI. Contributions in Kind

500. Noncash contributions are allowed in a company established in the classical method, i.e., through articles of association concluded before a notary public. In-kind contributions, as well as cash, must be made before the company is entered into the register. When submitting an application to register a company, the management board is required to attach a declaration of all members of the management board that the payments covering the share capital have been made in full to the notification.

501. Polish law allows for a very broad list of potential in-kind contributions. Despite initial doubts in the legal doctrine, it is widely accepted, among others, that it is permissible to contribute know-how, and industrial property rights, such as a patent, a right to a utility model or trademark protection right as an in-kind contribution. Shares in other companies can also be contributed, as can an enterprise belonging to the given shareholder.

VII. Other Material Formation Requirements

502. A limited liability company in formation is transformed into the appropriate company as soon as it is entered into the National Court Register. The entry is made by the registry court, at the request of the company in formation operating through the management board. Minor shortcomings when forming the company, which do not breach the public interest or the interests of the company, cannot constitute grounds for refusing to make the entry if remedying them were to be associated with excessively high costs.

§3. Essential Elements of the Legal Person: Seat, Name, Objects Clause and (In Some Civil Law Countries—Commercial or Civil) Character

503. A limited liability company may be formed for any legally permissible purpose.[103] Therefore, the company may be founded for business or nonbusiness purposes. Non-profit companies operated in the form of limited liability companies in Poland actually exist. Such companies would need to be financed from external sources, such as shareholders' contributions or additional contributions, or donations.

504. Of course, the vast majority of limited liability companies operating in Poland are established for business purposes.

505. The exception to the rule that a limited liability company may be established for any legally permissible purpose may arise from restrictions in specific regulations. For example, activities such as banking may only be conducted in the form of joint-stock companies. Additionally, only companies operated in the form of joint-stock companies may be listed on the stock exchange.

506. The name of the limited liability company can be chosen freely; it only needs to contain the company name with the use of the identification of a limited liability company. It is also admissible to use the abbreviation "Spółka z o.o." or "sp. z o.o."

507. A limited company has full legal personality. Therefore, it is a legal entity that is separate from its shareholders; it may acquire rights and incur obligations on its own behalf, sue and be sued.

508. Polish law contains general rules regarding the seat of all legal persons. The seat of a legal person is a town. Therefore, it is sufficient to specify the name of the town, e.g., Warsaw, Kraków or Wrocław. There is no need to specify the address in the given town in the articles of association. The address is only reported to the company's notification to the court register. The shareholders may choose the seat of a limited liability company at any time, with the reservation that it must be a town located in Poland. Most frequently, the partners specify the town where the management board operates as the company's seat. However, this is not necessary and it is possible to choose the company's seat according to other, additional criteria, such as the location of the main production plant, the place where services are provided by the company, or the place of residence of most of the members of the management board.

509. The company's seat indicated in the articles of association and subsequently disclosed in the register of entrepreneurs is of significant practical significance. It specifies, for instance, the territorial jurisdiction of the court when any

103. Article 151 §1 CCCP.

action is brought against the company. The registered office may also specify the default place of performing obligations. The company's seat also determines the properties of the administrative offices regarding the company's affairs, the most important of which are tax issues and affairs.

§4. Capital and Shares

I. Different Concepts of Capital

A. Nominal, Issued, Paid up, Minimum and Authorized Capital (A Subheading for Each)

510. The minimum share capital of a limited company is PLN 5,000, which is just over EUR 1,000.

II. Alteration of Capital Requirements

511. The share capital in a limited liability company may be both increased and decreased.

512. The share capital may be increased by increasing the nominal value of the existing shares or—much more often—by establishing new shares. More on this subject below.

III. Preferential Right of Subscription

513. In the event of an increase in the company's share capital, if new shares are created, the shareholders have the priority right to subscribe for new shares in proportion to their existing stake. This priority right is exercised at the request of the management board within one month. The priority right serves the purpose of preventing the dilution of the existing shareholders and their position in the company through the creation of new shares. They can therefore maintain their equity position in the company at the current level of increasing the objective values of the share capital.

514. As a rule, the acquisition of the shares by the existing shareholders, as in the case of new shareholders subscribing for shares and joining the company, requires the form of a notarial deed. This requirement does not apply if the increase arises from a resolution on the increase in capital passed with the use of the template in the ICT system.

515. The share capital may be increased either under the existing provisions of the articles of association or on the basis of a resolution of the shareholders on the amendment of the articles of association.[104]

516. The norm in Polish practice is to increase the share capital under the existing provisions of the articles of association. This requires the introduction of provisions into the original wording of the company's articles of association, specifying the maximum amount of share capital and the date of the increase. This deadline can also be set many years ahead. In such a case, the increase may be made in the future by a resolution of the shareholders or another body provided for in the articles of association, e.g., the management board or the supervisory board, passed within the framework of the articles of association. Such an increase in the share capital does not constitute an amendment to the articles of association.

517. However, if the articles of association do not provide for the ability to increase the share capital under the existing provisions of the articles of association, a resolution will need to be passed by the shareholders with a qualified majority of two-thirds of the votes and the subscription for shares by new or existing shareholders in the form of a notarial deed. However, there is an exception—in a situation in which the share capital is increased by a resolution to amend the articles of association through the allocation of funds from supplementary or reserve capital—the new shares are attributable to the existing shareholders in proportion to their existing stakes by law and do not require subscription.[105]

518. The entry of the increase into the register is constitutive, while the increase takes place at the time it is registered in the register of entrepreneurs.

519. The increase in capital is reported by the management board, which also attaches the resolution, the declaration on the subscription for the shares and the declaration on making the contribution.

IV. Forbidden Reductions of Capital and Acquisition of Shares by the Corporation Itself

520. The share capital in a limited liability company may be reduced after registering the company. This requires the performance of a number of activities. It is inadmissible to reduce the share capital below the bottom threshold of PLN 5,000.

521. The formal requirements, which must be met, to reduce the share capital are described precisely in the CCCP. It is not possible to informally reduce the share capital. Three activities will be necessary to effectively conduct the operation of reducing the share capital.

104. Article 257 CCCP.
105. Article 260 CCCP.

522. First of all, the shareholders need to pass a resolution on the reduction of the share capital. This resolution constitutes an amendment to the articles of association. For this reason, it is subject to stricter requirements than other resolutions. The increased formal requirements are primarily the need for a notary public to minute the resolution and its passage with a qualified majority of two-thirds of the votes cast. The articles of association may provide for stricter conditions for passing a resolution reducing the share capital, e.g., by specifying the need for a larger number of shareholders to vote.

523. A resolution on the reduction in the share capital is only not passed by the shareholders' meeting, but by the company's management board if it is reduced in connection with the so-called automatic redemption of shares. The reasons for this arrangement should be specified as early as in the original articles of association.

524. The next requirement is the so-called convocation procedure for creditors, which has the objective of safeguarding interests. It is based on the public announcement of a reduction in capital that is passed, a public call for creditors to raise objections to the reduction and the satisfaction or security of objecting creditors.[106]

525. The last formal requirement is the submission of a written reduction to the court register. The change will only be effective upon its entry into the court register. The entry of the reduction of the share capital into the court register is therefore a necessary condition for the effectiveness of this operation. The company's management board should make such a notification.

526. In principle, a company cannot acquire its own shares.

527. A company may also not subscribe for its own shares. In the Polish legal doctrine, this is explained by the need for the principle of protecting share capital. This is because the situation in which a company is its own shareholder would lead to the negation of the principle of the reality of the share capital accumulated on the basis of the contribution of shareholders. It would actually lead to a contribution being made as the company's contribution to its own share capital, for which the contribution is intended.[107]

528. There are exceptions to the prohibition of the company to acquire its own shares and to take them as security. They are as follows:

- The company may acquire its own shares by way of enforcement to satisfy the company's claims that cannot be satisfied from other assets.
- The company may acquire its own shares for the purpose of their redemption.
- In other cases specified in the respective regulations.

106. Article 264 CCCP.
107. Cf. K. Bilewska & A. Chłopecki, *Prawo Handlowe*, p. 117.

V. Classes of Shares

A. *Ordinary Shares*

529. The share capital in a limited liability company is divided into shares of an equal or unequal nominal value. The nominal value of the shares cannot be less than PLN 50.

530. The sum of the value of the shares corresponds to the value of the share capital.

531. The shares are attributable to the shareholders, whereas, if shares of unequal values are created, each shareholder may hold only one share. However, in the case of equal and indivisible shares (which is the norm), a shareholder may hold more than one share. Whether a shareholder may hold one or more shares is specified in the articles of association.

532. The shares in the share capital of a limited liability company reflect the rights and obligations of the shareholder in the company.

533. Participation in a limited liability company in the Polish model of a company assumes an intangible form, i.e., it is a right for which bearer documents cannot be issued on a personal order.

Register of Shareholders

534. Shares are recorded in the register of shareholders.[108] The register of shareholders constitutes the basis for determining who is a shareholder in the company and how many shares he holds. The register of shareholders is kept by the management board of a limited liability company. It discloses:

- the surname and forename, or name of the firm, the shareholder's seat and full address or address for electronic deliveries;
- the number and nominal value of the shares belonging to the shareholder;
- the establishment of a pledge or usufruct on the share and the exercise of voting rights by the pledgee and the user;
- all changes regarding the shareholders and their shares.

535. The register of shareholders can be viewed by any shareholder.

536. The list of shareholders authorized to exercise rights from shares, of which the most important is obviously the right to participate in the voting on resolutions at the shareholders' meeting, is determined on the basis of the register of shareholders.

---

108. Article 188 CCCP.

B. Preferred Stock

537. In principle, the shares in a limited liability company are equal for all shareholders. Differences may arise from the provisions of an act of law or the articles of association.[109]

538. The articles of association of a limited liability company may provide for a preference of a share by assigning it special rights in the articles of association.

C. Non-voting

539. Each shareholder must have at least one vote in a limited company.

D. Multiple Voting

540. As mentioned above, the shares in a limited liability company are, in principle, equal. However, it is possible to give preference to a share by giving preferences in voting rights. The law allows for two or a maximum of three votes per share instead of one. Such preference is only possible in the case of shares of an equal nominal value.

E. Preference Shares with Regard to the Dividend

541. As mentioned above, the shares are, in principle, equal. It is possible to make shares preferred both on the basis of the provisions of the Act and on the basis of the decisions of the shareholders, which are reflected in the articles of association. One of the possible forms of making shares preferential applies to the preference regarding the dividend. However, this cannot exceed 150% of the dividend granted to non-preference shares.

F. Preference Shares Regarding the Liquidation Amount

542. It is also possible to give preference to shares in the method of participation in the application of assets in the event of a company's liquidation. The shareholders holding such shares will take part in the distribution of the amount paid in the event of the liquidation of the company with specific preferences over all other shareholders.

109. Article 174 CCCP.

VI. Transfer of shares

A. Admissibility

543. The sale of shares and the pledging of shares are, in principle, permissible at any time.

B. Form of Disposal of the Shares

544. The disposal of the shares must be made in writing with notarized signatures.[110] This is a special form of making declarations and concluding agreements in Polish law. It is a qualified form of the ordinary written form but is simultaneously less formal than the form of an agreement or declaration made in the form of a notarial deed. The difference in practice between the two forms is that, in the case of an agreement concluded with a notarized signature, only the identity of the signatory is notarized, but the notary public does not prepare the whole of the wording of the agreement or declaration, as is the case with the agreement or declaration made in the form of a notarial deed. In practice however, in Poland, in view of the ethical principles of practicing the profession of a notary public, notaries check the content of the whole of the agreement or declaration, including those that are submitted only in the form with a notarized signature. Therefore, it will be unacceptable to make a declaration in a language that is not known to the notary public without a translator and sign it in the presence of a notary public. Therefore, if share purchase agreements are also to be signed in the presence of a notary public, this must be prepared in Polish and, if they are prepared in a foreign language, a sworn translator of that language into Polish must be present at the signature of such an agreement.

545. In the case of a limited liability company, which was established electronically, the shares may also be sold using the template provided in the ICT system, while the seller's and buyer's declarations should have appropriate electronic signatures.

546. Polish law also allows for the transferability of some shares, as long as the articles of association allow a shareholder to have just one share. However, this should be specified in the articles of association.[111] Even so, the decided majority of limited liability companies registered in Poland have shares of an equal amount, while every shareholder may hold more than one share.

110. Article 180 §1 CCCP.
111. Article 181 CCCP.

C. Limitations

547. The CCCP allows the articles of association to make the sale of shares contingent on the company's consent or to be otherwise limited. The principles regarding a limitation of this type should be specified in the articles of association. Unless otherwise specified in the articles of association, the following principles apply: consent is given by the management board in writing. If consent is refused, the court may allow for the disposal if there are valid reasons. In the latter case, the company may present another buyer within the deadline specified by the registry court. In the event of a disagreement, the purchase price and payment term are set by the registry court at the request of a shareholder or the company, after obtaining an expert opinion if necessary. The shareholder can only freely dispose of his shares if the person specified by the company fails to pay the purchase price within the prescribed period unless he does not accept the payment offered.

D. Special Procedures of Sale and Purchase of Shares

548. A shareholder may also be changed in a limited liability company in a manner other than the normal procedure.

549. The special procedures of selling shares include, for example, the acquisition of shares by an heir. However, the assumption of the place of the deceased shareholder by his heirs can be ruled out or limited in the articles of association. However, the conditions for paying off the heirs must simultaneously be specified.[112]

550. If no restrictions have been introduced on the inheritance of the share, the acquisition takes place in accordance with the rules on inheritance. If several people are jointly entitled to one share, they exercise their rights in the company through a joint representative.

551. Acquisition by spouses is also a special procedure of purchase. According to the view presented by the majority of the doctrine on commercial law in Poland, if spouses have joint marital ownership and when one of them acquires a share of the funds arising from the joint marital ownership, he becomes a shareholder in the company, while the other spouse is entitled to participate in this joint ownership on the basis of surrogacy.[113] However, some authors go further and believe that the

112. Article 183 CCCP.

113. Cf., among others, K. Bilewska & A. Chłopecki, *Prawo handlowe*, p. 116; A. Koch & J. Napierała, *Prawo …*, pp. 374–375; A. Kidyba, *Kodeks spółek handlowych tom I, komentarz do art 1–300* [eng. *Code of Commercial Companies and Partnerships Volume 1, Commentary on Articles 1–300*], Warsaw 2017, p. 829. Similarly, also the judgments in Poland—cf. Supreme Court—among others, the judgment of the Supreme Court of May 20, 1999, I CKN 1146/97.

other spouse, who did not participate in the transaction and was not a party to the share purchase agreement, also becomes a shareholder in the commercial company.

552. In my opinion, the view is that only the spouse who acquired the share is the shareholder, even if he did so from funds originating from the joint ownership. An attempt to give primacy in this respect to the rules of family law and their orthodox interpretation would cause practical problems that are difficult to master—what would happen if both spouses came to the shareholders' meeting and each of them wanted to vote differently?

E. Registration

553. The disposal of shares is effective as soon as the company receives the notice from one of the interested parties, together with proof of the share being transferred.[114] The management board is obliged to make an entry into the register of shareholders on the basis of this notice.

554. The management board submits the new list of shareholders signed by all members of the management board to the registry court after every change in the membership of the shareholders.

VII. (Mortgage) Debentures and Other Securities Which Do Not (Yet) Represent Capital

555. A share of a limited liability company may be encumbered with a pledge. The establishment of a pledge is effective on the company at the time of notification by one of the interested parties and the provision of evidence of the establishment of the pledge. Information on the establishment of the pledge is entered into the register of shareholders.

556. Pledgees may exercise voting rights if the articles of association allow for this and the shareholder and pledgee so decide. The fact that the pledgee exercises voting rights is entered in the register of shareholders.

557. Similar rules apply to the right of usufruct.

114. Article 187 §1 CCCP.

§5. SHAREHOLDERS, MANAGEMENT AND CONTROL

I. Shareholder Control Mechanisms/Shareholders

A. Shareholders Meeting (Kinds, Convening, Proxies, Powers)

558. All the shareholders form a governing body of the company, which is the general meeting of shareholders. Shareholders have the right but not the obligation to participate in the work of the general meeting of shareholders.

559. Shareholders may participate in the general meeting personally or through representatives. Restrictions on this may be included in the articles of association. The power of attorney to vote should be granted in writing, otherwise null and void, and attached to the register of minutes. Neither a member of the management board nor an employee of the company may be proxies of shareholders at the general meeting of shareholders.

560. Resolutions may be passed both at and outside the general meeting of shareholders. In a limited liability company, it is therefore possible for shareholders to pass resolutions not as the general meeting of shareholders, as a governing body, but in the form of declarations of intent of the shareholders outside that body.

561. General meetings of shareholders are divided into annual and extraordinary.

562. The annual general meeting deals with matters that must be considered at the company at least once a year.

563. Both the extraordinary and annual general meeting may be held as a result of the correct notification of the shareholders, but also when all the share capital is represented at the meeting and nobody present raises any objections to the meeting being held or to individual matters being included on the agenda.[115]

564. An annual general meeting should be held within six months of the end of the financial year. The objectives of the annual general meeting are:

- to review and approve the management report on the company's activities, as well as the financial statements for the previous financial year;
- to pass a resolution on the distribution of the profit or the coverage of the loss if the articles of association do not rule out these matters from the competence of the general meeting of shareholders;
- to award a vote of approval to the company's governing bodies, namely the management board, the supervisory board and the audit committee, for the performance of their duties.

---

115. Article 240 CCCP.

565. Voting in writing is ruled out in matters that are considered at the annual general meeting.

566. However, any matters other than those mentioned above may also be discussed at the annual general meeting.

567. All general meetings that are not annual are extraordinary general meetings. In practice, all general meetings, except for annual general meetings which are held once a year, are extraordinary general meetings. Therefore, the name is somewhat misleading because it is most frequently about meetings at which decisions are made on current, ordinary matters that are not extraordinary matters.

B. Majority Rule: Legal and Statutory Protection of the Minority and Majority

568. Voting in general meetings takes place with shares. The general meeting passes resolutions, calculating the number of votes according to the number of shares held in the share capital. As mentioned above, the rule is that one vote is attributed to every share of an equal nominal value, unless the articles provide otherwise.

569. The principle is that resolutions are adopted with an absolute majority of votes cast.[116] This means that it will be sufficient to pass a resolution if the number of votes in favor is greater than half of the validly cast votes. In such a case, the abstentions are treated as if they were cast against the resolution.

570. In some cases, a resolution needs to be passed with a qualified majority. In many regulations, the CCCP introduces exceptions to the general rule of passing resolutions with an absolute majority. The key is the requirement to pass a resolution with a two-thirds majority of the votes cast on the following matters:

- the amendment of the articles of association;
- the merger of companies;
- the dissolution of a company;
- the disposal of the enterprise or a standalone part of the enterprise.

571. In turn, a resolution on a material change in the company's business requires a three-quarters majority of votes.[117]

572. And finally, in the case of resolutions introducing amendments to the articles of association, in which the shareholders' benefits are increased or their rights from shares are reduced or awarded personally to individual shareholders, the consent of all shareholders to whom these resolutions apply is required.[118]

---

116. Article 245 CCCP.
117. Article 246 §1 CCCP.
118. Article 246 §3 CCCP.

573. When calculating an absolute or qualified majority, with an even number of votes cast, the method of counting votes is not difficult. In the case of an odd number of votes, the fraction is rounded up to the nearest full natural number.[119]

574. Modifications to these principles can arise from the articles of association. Therefore, the articles of association may, for example, provide for a qualified majority other than specified above, or provide that resolutions, which may be passed in other companies with an absolute majority of votes, will require a qualified majority in the given company. It is unacceptable to introduce a rule into the articles of association that resolutions requiring a qualified majority of votes in accordance with the CCCP may be passed by an ordinary or absolute majority.

575. If the articles of association do not require a quorum, the general meeting will be valid regardless of the number of shares represented. However, if the articles of association specify a certain number of represented shares, which are necessary for the validity of the meeting, the resolution will only be valid if the quorum has been achieved. The Polish legal doctrine considers that, if a shareholder leaves the meeting during the deliberations and the resulting decline in the representation of shares to below the limit set for the validity of the meeting (quorum) does not allow for resolutions to be passed, even if the shares of the shareholders remaining at the meeting gave a sufficient majority to pass the resolution, as provided for in the articles of association.[120]

C. Annual Accounts and Report; Profits and Dividends

576. The shareholders decide on the distribution of profit by way of a resolution which should be passed at a so-called annual general meeting of shareholders (discussed above).

D. Control by Individual Shareholders

577. Shareholders can exercise individual control primarily through the ability to question the resolutions passed by the company. Polish law provides for two procedures for contesting resolutions. The first of these is an action to annul a resolution. The second is an action to declare a resolution invalid.

578. The action to annul a resolution may be filed when a resolution of the shareholders is in conflict with the articles of association or good practices and simultaneously breaches the company's interests of the company or has the objective of causing injury to a shareholder. An action to annul a resolution may be filed within one month of learning of the resolution, no later than six months from the

119. Cf. A. Kidyba, *Prawo* … , p. 451.
120. Cf. A. Kidyba, *Prawo* … , p. 451 and decision of the Supreme Court of Jan. 22, 1993, I CRM 2014/92.

date on which the resolution is passed. Contesting a resolution does not suspend the registration proceedings; the passage of resolutions is subject to registration. However, the registry court may order a stay of the proceedings after conducting a hearing.

579. In turn, an action may be filed to declare a resolution invalid. If a shareholder finds that the resolution breaches a provision of the unconditionally applicable law, it may file for the resolution to be held invalid. This is a special type of action for establishment. The court judgment declaring the resolution invalid will be of a constitutive nature. Therefore, the claimants filing the action in this procedure are not interested in the annulment of the resolution, but in declaring that the given resolution is invalid.

580. It should be emphasized that in accordance with the view that is generally accepted in the Polish legal doctrine, an action to find a resolution invalid can only be filed in the procedure of the CCCP, which restricts both the group of entities authorized to file such a motion and the deadline within which such an action may be filed (this will be discussed further below). It is inadmissible to use the general legal basis specified in the Civil Procedures Code (CPC) regarding an action for establishment.[121]

581. Other than the shareholders, the governing bodies and the members of those governing bodies, namely, for instance, the members of the management board, will be entitled to bring an action to set aside a resolution and declare it invalid. A shareholder who is present at the meeting and wants to contest the resolution must vote against the resolution and, after it is passed, request that his objection be minuted. Shareholders also have the right to appeal against resolutions if they have been unreasonably not admitted to take part in general meetings of shareholders.[122] It is also stated in the doctrine that, if a break is ordered which was not included in the agenda, this is never provided for by the articles of association, so it can be concluded that this is the unreasonable prevention of shareholders participating in general meetings.[123]

582. Regardless of contesting resolutions through actions to declare a resolution invalid or to annul a resolution in a limited liability company, the shareholder is entitled to exercise individual control over the company's affairs. This is one of the elements that bring a limited liability company closer to partnerships. The right of personal control is not a right awarded to individual shareholders in the articles of association; it arises directly from the nature of the company and the law itself. Every shareholder has the right of control.

583. Under the right of control, every shareholder may review the company's ledgers and documents at any time, prepare a balance sheet for his own use or

121. Article 189 CPC.
122. Article 250 CCCP.
123. Cf. A. Kidyba, *Prawo* ..., p. 453.

request explanations from the management board. However, the articles of association can rule out the right of individual control of a company if a supervisory board or audit committee has been appointed at the company. The company's management board can refuse to provide explanations and make the company's ledgers and documents available to the shareholder for review if there is reasonable concern that the shareholder will use them for purposes which are in conflict with the company's interests and will therefore cause significant damage to the company.

584. A shareholder, who has been denied the right to review the company's documents or ledgers, may submit a petition to the registry court to obligate the management board to provide explanations or make the company's documents or ledgers available for review.

E. Control by the Supervisory Board

585. The appointment of a supervisory body in a limited liability company, such as an audit committee or supervisory board is optional. The obligation to establish one of these bodies arises when:

- the articles of association provide for this;
- there are more than twenty-five shareholders and the share capital is more than PLN 500,000;
- the company was established from the transformation of a municipal plant or a municipal enterprise into a company with the municipality as the sole shareholder;
- the company was established from the transformation of a state-owned enterprise into a company in which the Treasury is the sole shareholder and the right of individual control is ruled out;
- special provisions provide for this.[124]

586. An audit committee and a supervisory board may be simultaneously appointed.[125]

587. If the company has an audit committee, the supervisory board will only have a supervisory function. If an audit committee has not been appointed but a supervisory board has, the supervisory board deals with both supervision and audit. The regulations contain an example of the powers of the supervisory board in a limited liability company. It includes:

- constant supervision over the company's business in all areas of its activities;
- the assessment of the management report on the company's activities, as well as the financial statements for the previous financial year;

---

124. According to A. Kidyba, *Prawo* …, p. 436.
125. Article 213 §1 CCCP.

– the assessment of the management board's motions on profit distribution or the offset of losses;
– the submission to the general meeting of shareholders of an annual written report on the assessment of the results referred to in the above points.

588. It is simultaneously possible to increase the rights of the audit commission in excess of the above examples of powers.[126] Of the most common ones encountered in practice, it is worth mentioning the ability to make the validity of certain activities undertaken by the management board contingent on the receipt of consent from the supervisory board.

II. Administrative or Management Body

A. Management Board (Appointment Requirements, Remuneration, Dismissal)

589. The management board is a body with management and representation powers and responsibilities. Every limited company necessarily has a management board.

590. Only natural persons may be members of the management board. They may be either shareholders or people from outside the group of shareholders.

591. The management board may be either single- or multiple-person.

592. The rule is that the management board is appointed by the shareholders by resolution. However, the articles of association may provide otherwise. For example, it is possible to specify in the articles of association that the management board will be appointed by the supervisory board or that individual members of the management board will be appointed directly by the shareholders.

B. Powers of Management and Representation

593. The management board's powers include representation and handling the company's affairs. The scope of a management board member's right of representation encompasses all activities in court and out of court. Only the disposal and lease of the business or its separable standalone part or the establishment of limited rights in rem over it requires a resolution of the shareholders.

594. Only in certain situations does the management board not have the power to represent the company. This applies to agreements and disputes between the company and the members of the management board, as well as disputes regarding the

126. Article 220 CCCP.

annulment of resolutions or holding resolutions invalid. The company is represented by the supervisory board or proxies appointed by a resolution of the shareholders in agreements and disputes between the company and the members of the management board.[127]

595. Every member of the management board may have the right to represent the limited liability company individually, but it is also possible to introduce the principle of joint representation by two or more members of the management board. How it will be in a given company should arise from the articles of association.

596. In some situations, the consent of a body other than the company's management board is required for a company to effectively conclude an agreement. The effectiveness of an agreement concluded without such consent depends on whether the need to obtain consent to conclude the given agreement arises from the articles of association and therefore the decisions of the shareholders themselves, or by a requirement provided for by law. In the latter case, an activity concluded without the required consent will be invalid, whereas if consent is required only because it is provided for in the articles of association, a legal transaction concluded without the required consent will be valid, but the members of the management board expose themselves to liability for overstepping their powers.

C. Duties of Members of the Management Board to the Company (Conflict of Interest) the Shareholders and Third Parties

597. In a limited liability company, the principles of loyalty apply to board members (the shareholders have no obligation to be loyal to the company). The scope of the noncompetition clause has been specified directly in the CCCP.

598. First of all, the members of the management board are prohibited from engaging in competing interests with the company. The prohibition to engage in competing interests means the prohibition to conduct the same type of business as the business of the company in which that person is a member of the board that is entered into the register in their own or someone else's name, directly or through others.

599. Second, the members of the management board are prohibited from participating in a competitive company as a partner in a civil partnership or other partnership or a member of a governing body of a company, or participating in a competitive legal person as a member of a governing body.

127. Article 210 CCCP.

600. Third, the members of the management board are prohibited from participating in a company if the member of the management board holds at least 10% of the stocks or shares in that company or has the right to appoint at least one member of its management board.[128]

601. Unless the articles of association provide otherwise, permits for the members of the management board to conduct competitive activities are granted by the bodies authorized to appoint the management board,

D. Liability of the Management Board Members

602. The rules on both civil and criminal liability of the members of the management board in both a limited company and a joint-stock company have been regulated extensively in Polish law.

603. The members of the management board bear civil liability with respect to creditors, the company and the shareholders. The members of the management board are jointly and severally liable with the company to the creditors if the management board makes a declaration that the contributions have been made in full and the data in that declaration is false. The members of the management board will also be liable to creditors in the event of the submission of false data when registering an increase in the share capital.

604. The key regulations regarding the liability of the members of the management board apply to a situation in which the company is insolvent. If enforcement against the company proves unsuccessful, the members of the management board are jointly and severally liable for the company's liabilities. This liability depends exclusively on the results of the enforcement conducted against the company. Therefore, it is irrelevant that a member of the management board took part in the assumption of the liability that ultimately led to the ineffectiveness of the enforcement. This is a personal responsibility, which is unlimited, joint and several.[129]

605. A member of the management board may be released from the personal liability specified above if he shows that bankruptcy has been declared at the appropriate time or that a decision has been issued at the right time to open restructuring proceedings or to approve an arrangement in proceedings regarding the approval of the arrangement. A member of the management board may also be released from this liability if he demonstrates that the failure to file for bankruptcy did not take place through his fault, or in a situation where the creditor did not suffer any damage, despite the failure to file for bankruptcy or a decision not being issued to open a restructuring procedure or the failure to approve an arrangement in proceedings regarding the approval of the arrangement.[130] In practice, it is very difficult to prove

128. Article 211 §1 CCCP.
129. Article 299 §1 CCCP.
130. Article 299 §2 CCCP.

one of these last two premises while the members of the management board are essentially required to ensure that a motion is filed for bankruptcy at the appropriate time.

606. Additionally, the members of the management board are liable to the company for the emergence of a liability or for damage.

607. In turn, the criminal liability of the members of the management board applies to a situation of acting to the detriment of the company, presenting or declaring false data and failing to comply with accounting and bookkeeping obligations.

III. Auditor (Appointment, Powers, Duties)

608. The appointment of an auditor requires a decision of the respective authorities of the company.

IV. Workers' Participation (E.g., Via Two-Tier Board Structure or Auditor Appointment) Left Blank

609. Polish commercial law does not provide for obligatory employee participation in the management or supervision of the company. Employee representatives are guaranteed a certain period of time on supervisory boards of companies which are appointed in the process of commercialization (transformation) of state-owned enterprises.

§6. Liquidation of the Company

I. Grounds for Winding-Up (Court Decision, Shareholders' Meeting)

610. The company is dissolved as a result of the principles set out in the regulations or in the articles of association. The basic reasons for dissolving a company are both reasons that result in the automatic dissolution of the company, as well as those that require a court decision.

611. The first of these reasons that automatically cause the dissolution of the company, if they arise, include the passage of a resolution on the dissolution of the company, the declaration of the company's bankruptcy and several other reasons specified in special acts of law.

612. In turn, the reasons that require a court ruling include situations where a company is dissolved as a result of a request of a shareholder or a member of the governing body if the company's objective becomes unachievable or other important reasons have arisen. The dissolution of a company as a result of a petition of a state authority if the company's activities breach the law or threaten a public interest is also of such a nature.[131]

II. The Effect of Winding-Up: Liquidation

613. The result of the dissolution is the opening of the company's liquidation. This will only be different if the company is declared bankrupt—then bankruptcy proceedings are conducted.

614. Liquidation has the intention of ending the company's activities serving the purpose of satisfying the interests of the company's creditors.

615. In principle, at the time of liquidation, new cases may only be taken up if this is required for ending pending cases.

616. During liquidation, profit may not be distributed to the shareholders nor may the assets be divided before paying off all the creditors.[132]

617. Liquidation activities include the termination of the company's current business, the collection of claims, the fulfillment of the company's obligations and the liquidation of the company's assets.

618. The supplement "*w likwidacji*" [under liquidation] should be included in the name of a company that is in liquidation.

619. The liquidation is conducted by the liquidators. In principle, unless the articles of association or a resolution of the shareholders provide otherwise, the liquidators are the members of the management board. The court only nominates the liquidators if the court decides to on the dissolution of the company. The provisions on the members of the management board apply to the liquidators. The liquidators have the right to handle the company's affairs and represent it.[133]

620. The regulations list the basic activities that they should also perform. They are as follows:

- Reporting the opening of the liquidation to the court by the given liquidators.
- The announcement of the dissolution of the company and the opening of liquidation, calling on the creditors to report their claims.

131. Article 271 CCCP.
132. Article 275 §2 CCCP.
133. Article 276 CCCP.

- Preparation of the liquidation opening balance sheet and the annual report on activities which should be presented for approval by the general meeting; performance of the basic liquidation activities, such as ending the company's business, collecting claims, performing liabilities and liquidating the company's assets.
- In addition to satisfying or securing creditors, the liquidators should divide the assets that remain among the shareholders in proportion to their stakes.
- The presentation of the financial statements as at the day preceding the distribution of the assets remaining after satisfying or securing the creditors among the shareholders for approval by the general meeting.
- The announcement of the approved liquidation report at the company's headquarters.
- Submission of a motion to remove the company from the register.

621. The completion of liquidation results in the submission of a motion to the register to remove the company and the decision on the removal. This ends the company's legal existence.

622. It should also be openly stated that the liquidation procedure of limited liability companies in Poland is rather complicated and formalistic. Consequently, there are hundreds of thousands of zombie companies on the market—namely, those that no longer conduct any business, have no governing bodies, but are formally not liquidated and are still registered in the register of entrepreneurs.

§7. Mergers and Takeovers

623. Please *see the* chapter on mergers and divisions of partnerships, companies and corporation.

§8. Holding Companies and Subsidiaries

624. A limited liability company may be established so it can earn an income from its participation in other entities. The activities of such a company may be limited exclusively to making contributions to another company in which it is a shareholder. Such a limited liability company would therefore receive an income not so much from running its own business, but rather from receiving payments from the profit of other legal persons. As is commonly accepted in the Polish literature, it is also permissible to establish a limited company to manage a holding company.[134]

625. In addition, the provisions of Polish law contain regulations regarding holding company law. Some of these rules not only apply to limited liability companies

134. Cf. A. Koch & J. Napierała, *Prawo …* , pp. 336–337 and A. Szajkowski & M. Tarska (in:) S. Sołtysiński, et al., *Kodeks spółek handlowych, Volume 2, Spółka z ograniczona odpowiedzialnością. Komentarz do artykułów 151–300* [eng. *Code of Commercial Companies and Partnerships, Volume 2, Limited Liability Company. Commentary on Articles 151–300*], Warsaw 2014, p. 15.

but also to other entities, including cooperatives or foundations. Some of them only apply to commercial companies, while others to companies and partnerships, while excluding other entities.

626. The basic regulations can be found in the CCCP. It applies to the basis of the regulations regarding holding company dependencies. The Code regulated the concepts of parent company, subsidiary and the concept of an affiliate. The parent company is a commercial company if:

- it directly or indirectly has the majority of votes at the general meeting including as a pledgee or user, or in the management board of another company (subsidiary), including on the basis of agreements with other persons; or
- it is entitled to appoint or dismiss the majority of members of the management board of another company (subsidiary) or cooperative (subsidiary cooperative), including under agreements with other persons; or
- the members of its management board constitute more than half the members of the management board of another company (subsidiary) or cooperative (subsidiary cooperative); it directly or indirectly has the majority of votes in a subsidiary partnership or at the general meeting of a subsidiary cooperative, including on the basis of agreements with other persons; or
- it exerts a decisive influence on the activities of a subsidiary or a subsidiary cooperative, in particular on the basis of agreements on the management of the subsidiary.[135]

627. If two commercial companies have the majority of each other's votes calculated in accordance with the principles set out above, the commercial company which has the higher percentage of votes at the other company's general meeting is considered the parent company. However, if each of the companies were to have an equal percentage of votes at the other company's general meeting, the parent company would be the company that exerts an influence on the subsidiary on the basis of any of the other connections specified above.[136]

628. In turn, an affiliate is a company in which another commercial company or cooperative directly or indirectly holds at least 20% of the votes at the general meeting, including as a pledgee or usufructuary, or on the basis of an agreement with other persons, or which directly holds at least 20% of the shares in the other company.[137]

629. Polish law has sparse regulations on the obligations of parent companies with respect to subsidiaries. One of the obligations is the obligation of the parent company to notify the subsidiary of the existence of a relationship of dominance. Such a notification should be sent to the subsidiary within two weeks of the date of the emergence of this relationship. The sanction for failing to do so would be the

135. Article 4 §4 CCCP.
136. Cf. A. Kidyba, *Prawo* ..., pp. 260–261.
137. Article 4 §5 CCCP.

suspension of voting rights from the shares of the parent company representing more than 33% of the subsidiary's share capital.

630. Additionally, the shareholders, as well as the members of the management board or supervisory board of a company may request that a commercial company, which is a shareholder in that company, provides information as to whether it is a parent or affiliate of the commercial company or cooperative requesting the information, or the shareholders of that same company. Such an authorized person may also request the disclosure of the number of shares or votes which the commercial company that was asked the question has in the company in which it participates, including as a pledgee, usufructuary or under agreements with other persons. Such requests for information and the responses should be submitted in writing. The responses should be given to the authorized person and the appropriate company within ten days of the date of receipt of the request. Importantly, the company that is required to respond must not exercise the rights from the shares in the company in which the authorized persons are participating from the date of the start of the countdown to the deadline for responding to the date on which the response is given.[138]

631. Sparse regulations on holding companies, including autonomous definitions of subsidiaries and parent companies, have been included in the regulations on competition and consumer protection.

§9. Taxation of Companies and Shareholders

632. A limited liability company is a payer of CIT on the same principles as a joint-stock company.

633. A limited liability company is also a remitter of VAT. Additionally, if a limited liability company has the status of a public benefit organization, organizational units of that company may be remitters, provided that they conduct business activities and independently prepare financial statements.

138. Article 6 §4 and §5 CCCP.

Part II. Partnerships

Chapter 1. General Partnership (Spółka Jawna)

§1. To What Extent Does This Type Enjoy Legal Personality?

634. Formally speaking, a partnership does not have legal personality. A general partnership may, however, acquire rights and assume liabilities, sue and be sued. It may acquire chattels and real property, conclude agreements on its own behalf, etc. In such a situation, the Polish legal system refers to having legal personality. From a practical point of view, the difference between legal personality and legal identity in the Polish legal system is negligible. Both of these categories of entities operate on the market independently, assuming liabilities on their own.

635. Such entities were once referred to in Poland as so-called imperfect legal persons. In other words, they are entities that appear independently in legal transactions while not having legal personality. It is currently unreasonable to talk about imperfect legal persons. Polish law distinguishes three types of entities: legal persons, natural persons and entities which have legal identity, of which a general partnership is one. All of them act on their own behalf.

636. A general partnership can be established in two ways. The first basic way is to establish a partnership from the beginning by concluding articles of partnership and making an entry in the Register of Entrepreneurs of the National Court Register. It is possible to establish a general partnership in the latter model including with the use of model articles of a general partnership, which includes completing electronic forms and sending the data in the ICT system to the relevant register of entrepreneurs. The second form is the transformation of a civil partnership into a general partnership.

637. The articles of partnership are first concluded in the basic model of establishing a general partnership. The articles should be concluded in writing. The articles should specify at least the partners of the general partnership, specify the trade name and the partnership's seat, define the value of the contributions made by each partner and the objects of the partnership's business, as well as its duration if the partnership is established for a fixed period.[139]

139. Articles 23 and 25 CCCP.

638. The general partnership is then entered into the register of entrepreneurs of the National Court Register. The entry is constitutive and therefore the partnership is only established upon the entry being made into the register.

§2. Nature of the Unlimited Liability

639. Each of the partners is responsible for all of the partnership's liabilities with the whole of their personal property. The liability of the partners is unlimited, joint and several and subsidiary.[140]

640. The liability is unlimited, which means that each partner is liable with all of his property for the liabilities of the general partnership.

641. This liability is joint and several, which means that each partner is jointly and severally liable with the other partners and with the partnership. This is defined as so-called passive solidarity. Therefore, a creditor of the partnership may demand all or a part of the performance from all debtors jointly, from several of them or from each of them individually. The satisfaction of the creditor by any of the debtors releases the others.

642. The liability of the partners of a general partnership is also subsidiary. In the Polish legal system, this means that the partnership's creditor may conduct enforcement against a partner's assets only if the enforcement of the partnership's assets proves unsuccessful. It should be emphasized, however, that there is no obstacle to a creditor bringing an action against a partner before enforcement from the partnership's assets proves unsuccessful. The case law of the courts indicates the following options for a creditor of a general partnership to pursue claims:

(i) sue the partner together with the partnership and obtain an enforcement order against the partnership and the partner (except that, in the case of the partner, this is subject to subsidiarity, namely only if the enforcement against the partnership's assets is unsuccessful);
(ii) sue the partner separately from the partnership and obtain an enforcement order against the partner which is subject to subsidiarity;
(iii) sue a partner after the unsuccessful situations against the company and receipt of an enforcement order against him;
(iv) sue only the partnership and obtain an enforcement order against the company, followed by obtaining a *fiery facias* clause against the partner in the event of unsuccessful enforcement against the company partnership.[141]

140. Article 31 CCCP.
141. Cf. A. Koch & J. Napierała, *Prawo* ... .

§3. Contributions and Division of Profits

643. The assets of a general partnership constitute all property that has been contributed to it or acquired by the partnership during its existence. Therefore, assets contributed to the partnership as a contribution or acquired by the partnership constitute the partnership's own property.[142] Therefore, it is not the joint property of the partners, but the separate property of the partnership.

644. The contribution to the general partnership may be the transfer or encumbrance of ownership or other rights, as well as other benefits for the company.

645. If contributions are made to the company, they may be either cash or noncash contributions. In particular, property ownership rights and substantive rights, such as patent, trademark or proprietary copyrights may be noncash contributions. The provision of services or work to a general partnership may also be a contribution to the partnership. On the sideline, it can be mentioned that such a form of contribution is unacceptable in the case of companies, namely limited liability companies and joint-stock companies. However, if a contribution in the form of work is, in fact, being made to the company, the type of work and its value should be clearly stated in the articles of partnership. It should also be remembered that a contribution to the partnership in the form of work is not the same as the management of the partnership's affairs by partners, to which each partner is entitled, regardless of the type of contribution they bring to the partnership.

646. In a general partnership, each partner has the right to an equal share of the profits and losses, regardless of the type and value of the contribution. There are, however, exceptions to this rule. The partners may, in the articles of partnership, specify what the share of each of them will be in the profits and losses in any way. It is also possible to exclude some of the partners from participating in losses.[143] However, it is generally accepted in the Polish legal doctrine that it is inadmissible to rule out a partner's share of both profits and losses (so-called *societas leonina*) in the articles of partnership. Some representatives of the Polish legal doctrine go even further and believe that it is inadmissible to exclude a partner completely from participating in the profits.[144]

§4. Management

647. Polish law consistently distinguishes the notion of representation of the partnership from handling the partnership's affairs. Representation of the partnership is understood as making and accepting declarations of intent. However, handling the partnership's affairs encompasses the partnership's internal relations.

142. Article 28 CCCP.
143. Article 51 CCCP.
144. Cf. K. Bilewska & A. Chłopecki, *Prawo Handlowe.*

648. According to the provisions of the Polish CCCP, every partner of a general partnership has the right to represent that partnership. The partner's right to represent the partnership may be withdrawn in two cases. The first is the situation in which the articles of partnership provide for this (he must then agree to this). The second is when the court decides so.[145]

649. The partners may also agree and include in the articles of partnership that the partnership may be represented solely by at least two partners operating together, or by one partner together with a commercial representative. If such a provision is not included in the partnership's articles of partnership, each of them will be able to make declarations of intent on behalf of the partnership, receive declarations made to the partnership by other entities, and therefore in particular enter into contracts on behalf of the partnership.

650. Just as with any other company or partnership, a general partnership may also be represented by commercial representatives, proxies and liquidators.

651. Each of the partners not only has the right to represent a general partnership, but this right is also very broad—each partner can represent the partnership in all court and out-of-court activities, including the sale of real property and the sale of the partnership's business. In this respect, Polish law does not provide for any restrictions. Therefore, for example, the partners may actually agree and include a provision in the articles of partnership stating that some of them will not take steps of a specific type, although if these partners take such steps, this will be legally effective. No restrictions on the scope of representation to which the partners are entitled exert any legal effects externally, while activities performed despite such restrictions are valid and effective. At most, the partners who acted in conflict with the articles of partnership may be held liable for damages in the relations between the partners.

652. In turn, the management of the partnership's affairs applies to internal activities, and, in principle, the partners have complete freedom in this respect; they can stipulate any rules in the articles of partnership. If the partners do not decide on anything else, each of the partners will then have the right and obligation to handle the partnership's affairs, with the reservation that the partner may be deprived of the right and obligation to handle the partnership's affairs by way of a final court decision, for important reasons.

653. The partners handle the partnership's matters free of charge; they do not receive a fee for handling the partnership's affairs.

654. Unless the partners decide otherwise in the articles of partnership, the powers and responsibilities of the partners to handle the partnership's affairs differ by the category of matters being handled.

---

145. Articles 29 and 30 CCCP.

655. In the case of matters not exceeding the partnership's ordinary activities, each partner has the right to handle the partnership's affairs on his own, without a prior resolution of the partners, unless one of the other partners objects to this. A prior resolution of the partners is required in this latter situation, which is passed unanimously by the partners who have the right to handle the partnership's affairs (i.e., all partners by default).[146]

656. In turn, matters exceeding the partnership's ordinary activities require a resolution of all the partners, including those partners who are excluded from handling the partnership's affairs.

657. The last category of activities is that of the so-called urgent activities, which, if not performed, could cause serious damage to the partnership. Any partner handling the partnership's affairs can conduct urgent activities without a prior resolution, including when this act falls into the category of matters exceeding ordinary activities.[147]

658. It should also be noted that all partners have the obligation to refrain from any activity which is in conflict with the partnership's interests. Therefore, the partners cannot handle competing interests. The notion of a partnership's interest has not been defined in Polish law, but the provision specifies examples of competitive interests and explicitly mentions participation in a competitive partnership as a partner in a civil partnership or a general partnership or a shareholder, general partner or member of a governing body in the case of limited partnerships or companies. However, the competition prohibition may be canceled by the partners themselves.

§5. Transferability of Partnership Interests

659. The membership of partners in a general partnership may be changed.

660. First of all, partners can join the partnership. This requires the consent of all the partners.

661. Second, partners may also resign from the partnership.

662. Third, in Poland, it has also been possible for several years to transfer the rights and duties of a partner in a general partnership to another person. An existing partner may sell his rights and duties in a general partnership to another person if two conditions are satisfied. The first is the admission of such a possibility by the articles of partnership. This must be explicitly provided for. The next condition is the written consent of all other partners (unless the articles of partnership provide

146. Article 39 §2 and §3 CCCP.
147. Article 44 CCCP.

otherwise). However, if the articles of partnership were concluded using a template in the CIT system, the transfer of all rights and obligations is also possible using the appropriate template in that system.

663. In short, it can therefore be concluded that, in principle, all personal changes require unanimity of the existing partners of a general partnership.

§6. LIQUIDATION

664. Liquidation is the method of ending the activities of a general partnership. Legal and factual activities are conducted within the liquidation to liquidate the partnership's assets.

665. The reasons for the dissolution of the partnership resulting in the need to liquidate it are specified directly in the provisions of the law. These include the declaration of the partnership's bankruptcy, the death of a partner or the declaration of his bankruptcy, the termination of the articles of partnership by one of the partners, a unanimous resolution of all partners and the reasons provided for in the articles of partnership. However, it should be emphasized that, in the event of a partner's death or the declaration of his bankruptcy or the termination of the articles of partnership, the other partners may decide that the partnership is to continue to exist and not to liquidate the partnership.[148]

666. In principle, all the partners are the liquidators. There are, however, exceptions to this principle. The partners themselves may, by way of a unanimous resolution, appoint only certain partners or people from outside this group as liquidators. Likewise, a court may appoint only certain partners or people from outside this group as liquidators for important reasons, at the request of a partner or another person with a legal interest. In turn, in the case of bankruptcy, the liquidator will be replaced by a receiver.

667. Liquidators have extensive powers. Their obligations include conducting liquidation proceedings, managing the partnership's affairs and representing the partnership, as well as announcing the opening and the end of the liquidation, as well as submitting the motion to remove the partnership from the register.[149]

668. The mere fact of starting the liquidation proceedings should be disclosed to the partnership's trading partners and third parties. The partnership should use the name with the additional identification of "*w likwidacji*" [under liquidation].

669. The ultimate objective of liquidation is to liquidate the partnership's assets, which is possible after previously ending the current interests, performing the obligations and collecting the debts. It is not clearly prejudged in Polish law whether

148. Articles 58 and 64 CCCP.
149. Articles 77 §1, 78 §1, 81 and 84 §1 CCCP.

the liquidation may be ended and the partnership removed from the register in a situation in which it has contractual long-term obligations which have not been terminated or ended. Some representatives of the Polish legal doctrine are of the opinion that the partnership can still be liquidated in such a situation. The opponents of this concept believe that, from the point of view of the protection of creditors (trading partners who have concluded such long-term agreements with the partnership), the partnership cannot be liquidated until the agreement ends.

§7. Taxation (In Brief)

670. A general partnership is a taxpayer of CIT. Consequently, the partners of the general partnership are taxable with personal income tax.

671. Personal income tax is a direct tax—it is collected directly on the income. The tax is an income to the state budget. For the first time in 2022, income from CIT was higher than income from personal income tax.

672. Less than half of the personal income tax remains in the state budget, while more than half of the amount collected is paid to the local authority budgets.

673. All shareholders of a joint-stock company who are natural persons are taxpayers of personal income tax. The principle of residency, which is conditional on the place where the natural person is domiciled, is applicable. If natural persons have their place of residence in Poland, they are taxable on all their income (including that obtained from conducting business in Poland) regardless of the location of the sources of income. This is so-called unlimited tax liability.

674. The basis for taxation with personal income tax is the sum of income from individual sources of income. In turn, income is the positive difference between the sum of revenues and the costs of generating them in the given tax year.

675. The basic tax scale in personal income tax only encompasses taxable income on general principles. This is a progressive tax in Poland but in a mild form. Two tax rates apply: 12% and 32%. The tax rate was reduced in 2022 from 17% to 12%. In fact, young people are exempt from this tax—taxpayers who are under the age of 26 do not pay personal income tax on their income from service, employment or personal service contracts (up to approximately EUR 20,000 of revenue per year).

676. The tax-free amounts are still very low in Poland.

677. A whole range of special solutions has been provided for in personal income tax with regard to the situation of specific people. For example, the ability of spouses to make joint settlements, numerous tax exemptions (over a hundred different subject-related exemptions), and the ability to use the simplified form of taxation of a tax card can be mentioned.

678. An extremely important possibility in practice is the ability to make a settlement of income from business activities, including from business conducted by commercial law companies, in the form of a flat rate tax. The tax rate is then 19%. No tax-free amount applies. The 19% rate applies regardless of the amount of income earned by the taxpayer. It is not possible to make joint settlements with the spouse.

679. In the case of the liability of partners of a partnership—a general partnership, professional partnership and general partners in limited partnerships or limited joint-stock partnerships, as well as partners in civil partnerships—they are jointly and severally liable with the partnership and the other partners for the partnership's tax arrears constituting a result of the partnership's activities. The same rule applies to the liability of a former partner for tax arrears from obligations, the payment term of which passed while he was a partner.

680. Furthermore, a general partnership is also a remitter of VAT.

Chapter 2. Limited Partnership

§1. To What Extent Does This Type Enjoy Legal Personality?

681. Like a general partnership, a limited partnership does not formally have legal personality, but it has the attribute which is referred to in Polish law as legal identity. A limited partnership may therefore acquire real property and chattels on its own behalf, enter into agreements on its own behalf, and so on. It also has its own assets, which are separate from those of its partners.

§2. Establishment of the Partnership

682. Articles of partnership must be concluded and an entry must be made into the register of entrepreneurs in order to establish a limited partnership. The articles should be concluded in the form of a notarial deed. The articles of a limited partnership should contain at least the specification of the partners, indicating which of them is a general partner and which is a limited partner; the partnership's name and its seat, the objects of the partnership's business, the duration of the partnership if specified and the indication of the contributions made by each of the partners, their value, as well as the limited amount.[150]

683. The name of the limited partnership should include the name of one or more general partners. However, the name of the limited partnership must not include the names of the limited partners. In the case of non-compliance with this prohibition, the limited partner disclosed in the name of the partnership will be fully liable for the partnership's obligations as if he were a general partner and therefore without limitation.[151]

684. A limited partnership may also be established using the template of the articles made available in the IT system, namely in electronic mode.

§3. Nature of the Unlimited Liability

685. Liability in a limited partnership and the rules on liability are a key element that distinguishes a limited partnership from other commercial companies and partnerships in Polish law.

686. The partners described as general partners are responsible for the partnership's liabilities on the same principles as the partners of a general partnership. They are therefore responsible for the partnership's obligations to its creditors without limitation. This is liability for binding the partnership with the partner's personal

150. Article 105 CCCP.
151. Article 104 §4 CCCP.

property. This is unlimited, joint and several and subsidiary liability. More can be found on these concepts in the part on the liability of the partners of a general partnership.

687. However, the liability of the second category of partners, i.e., the limited partners, for the partnership's liabilities is different. Limited partners are liable for the liabilities of the partnership to its creditors in a limited manner. The level of the limited partner's liability with his personal property is equal to the difference between the limited amount and the value of the contribution made to the partnership.[152] As can be seen from this, the key concept here is the concept of the limited amount, while the concept of the contribution made is also important.

688. The limited amount under Polish law is the amount of the upper limit of a limited partner's liability with his personal property for the partnership's liabilities to its creditors. The limited partnership sum should be expressed in numerical terms in Polish zlotys. It has been accepted in the Polish legal doctrine that it is inadmissible to specify the level of the limited amount by specifying it in a currency other than zlotys.[153] It is also accepted in the legal doctrine that the limited amount should be specified at a certain minimum level without indicating exactly what minimum level would be acceptable. In my opinion, there are no obstacles for the limited amount to be set at a very low level.

689. It is possible to change the limited amount, but this will require an amendment to the articles of partnership.

690. However, a reduction in the limited amount has no legal effect on the creditors whose claims arose before such a reduction was entered into the register.[154]

691. As mentioned above, the limited partner is free of liability within the value of the contribution made to the partnership. The contribution should be valued at the time it is made to the partnership.

692. In the doctrine of Polish law, it has been rightly accepted that, if the partners accepted a contribution at a higher value than the actual value of the contribution, the actual, real value of the contribution would still be reliable for creditors. Therefore, if a limited partner made a contribution of PLN 50,000 to cover a contribution of PLN 100,000, he would be free of liability with his personal property only up to the amount of PLN 50,000, even if the value of the contribution in the limited partnership's internal ledgers is marked as being higher than its actual value. It is accepted In the Polish legal doctrine that, even in the event of an underestimation of the value of the contribution, the actual value of the contribution will be applicable. Therefore, if a limited partner makes a contribution of a real value of PLN 100,000 and is admitted into the partnership as having a value of only PLN

152. Articles 108, 111 and 112 CCCP.
153. Cf. A. Koch & J. Napierała, *Prawo* ..., p. 301.
154. Article 113 CCCP.

50,000, in the event of a subsequent increase in the limited amount to PLN 100,000, it should be accepted that the limited partner will be completely exempt from personal liability because he has made a contribution the actual value of which was precisely that PLN 100,000.[155]

693. In the event of a refund of the contribution, in whole or in part, the limited partner's liability with his personal property for the partnership's liabilities to its creditors is restored to an amount that is equal to the value of the refund made. Importantly, even in the case of a depletion of the partnership's assets through a loss, it is considered that any payment made by the partnership to the limited partner before supplementing the contribution to its original value specified in the articles of partnership is a refund of the contribution with respect to the creditors.

694. Additionally, anyone who joins the partnership as a limited partner is also liable for the partnership's liabilities that existed at the time he was entered into the register.[156] Therefore, according to the principles set out in the CCCP providing for the limited liability of a limited partner, the limited partner is only liable from the moment of joining the partnership. His liability is unlimited for earlier liabilities. From a practical point of view, anyone who intends to join a limited partnership as a limited partner should conduct a thorough due diligence study of the partnership's existing obligations.

§4. Contributions and Division of Profits

695. In a limited partnership, a limited partner, namely a partner whose liability is limited, participates in the partnership's profit in proportion to the actual contribution made to the partnership. However, the articles of partnership may introduce separateness in this respect. The profit attributable to a limited partner for a given financial year should first be allocated to supplement the contribution he actually made to the value of the contribution that was agreed and which is specified in the articles of partnership. The limited partner participates in the loss only up to the value of the agreed contribution, although other solutions are also possible, on condition that they are appropriately included in the articles of partnership.[157]

§5. Management

696. A limited partnership has two types of partners. At least one partner has unlimited liability for the partnership, while the liability of at least one is limited. Differences regarding the management of the limited partnership are also related to this.

---

155. Cf. A. Koch & J. Napierała, *Prawo* … p. 303.
156. Article 114 CCCP.
157. Article 123 CCCP.

697. When talking about managing the limited partnership, reference here should actually be made to the legal status of the limited partner and the general partner and this legal status should be discussed in terms of managing the partnership.

698. A general partner in a limited partnership can be either a natural person or a legal person or an entity that has legal identity, which therefore also includes partnerships. Consequently, limited partnerships may be established with limited liability companies as general partners in Poland. This form is especially popular not only in Germany but also appears relatively frequently in Poland.

699. The general partners represent the limited partnership unless they are deprived of the right to represent the partnership by the articles of partnership or a final court decision.[158] In fact, therefore, every general partner has the legally guaranteed right to represent the partnership. The scope of this right, as in the case of partners of a general partnership, has been broadly defined. A general partner can therefore represent a limited partnership in all of the partnership's court and out-of-court activities. The right to represent the partnership cannot be restricted by the effect on third parties. Therefore, it is inadmissible under Polish law to introduce restrictions regarding, for instance, the prohibition of individual general partners to conclude agreements of specific wording or of a specific value. It is only possible to agree in the articles of partnership that the general partners will be able to represent the partnership jointly as two or more people or together with a commercial representative.

700. The general partner may be deprived of the right to represent the partnership in the articles of partnership or by a final and binding judgment. In the latter case, this can only happen for important reasons.

701. General partners also have the right to handle the affairs of the partnership, and therefore to take up all activities in the partnership itself in the internal relations. The provisions on general partnerships apply here accordingly. I would therefore like to refer the reader to the relevant chapter on the general partnership. However, it should be emphasized that these provisions will only apply if the articles of partnership do not regulate these matters differently.

702. In turn, limited partners do not have the right to act on behalf of the partnership. They can only represent it as proxies.[159] A limited partner may be granted both a general power of attorney and a generic power of attorney or a power of attorney for specific activities. A limited partner may also be a commercial representative of a limited partnership.

703. A limited partner does not have the right or obligation to handle the partnership's affairs unless the articles of partnership provide otherwise. The limited

158. Article 117 CCCP.
159. Article 118 CCCP.

partner's consent is only required in matters exceeding the scope of the partnership's ordinary activities unless the articles of partnership provide otherwise.

704. In summary, therefore, it can be concluded that the default, statutory model of the operation of a limited partnership is one in which the general partners both represent the partnership externally and handle its affairs, while the role of the limited partner is limited to contributing funds or items to the partnership. However, the model is flexible enough to allow for far-reaching modifications. Consequently, a limited partnership can be formed, in which the general partner is a limited liability company, the shareholders of which are the limited partners. It is also possible to give a limited partner far-reaching rights to represent the partnership in the form of granting him a power of representation, as well as to give him the right to handle the affairs of the partnership through appropriate provisions in the articles of partnership.

§6. Transferability of Partnership Interests

705. The composition of the shareholders may be changed on similar principles to the case of a change in the composition of the partners in a general partnership. I would therefore like to refer the reader to the relevant subchapter on the general partnership. The differences only apply to certain situations related to limited partners. Therefore, in particular, the death of a limited partner does not constitute a reason for dissolving a limited partnership (unlike in the case of a general partner whose death constitutes a reason to dissolve a limited partnership).

§7. Liquidation

706. The liquidation of a limited partnership proceeds in a similar way to the liquidation of a general partnership. I would therefore like to refer the reader to the considerations in the relevant subchapter on the general partnership.

§8. Taxation (In Brief)

707. A limited partnership is not a taxpayer of CIT. The same principles that apply to partners of a general partnership who are natural persons, which I discussed above, are applicable.

708. Furthermore, a limited partnership is also a remitter of VAT.

Chapter 3. Professional Partnership

§1. To What Extent Does This Type Enjoy Legal Personality?

709. Like general and limited partnerships, a professional partnership has no legal personality but has a so-called legal identity. From a practical point of view, the differences between legal personality and identity are negligible. A partnership, like legal entities, may acquire rights and be a party to obligations. A professional partnership has its own assets, which are separate from those of its partners. It concludes agreements on its own behalf. She can sue and be sued.

§2. Establishment of the Partnership

710. A professional partnership can only be established by professionals and only if this is mentioned in the relevant provision on the professional partnership.

711. Various concepts clashed at the stage of establishing the CCCP. In particular, consideration was given to whether a general definition of a profession should be introduced into the CCCP when introducing this Code into Polish law. This did not happen. However, certain features can be accepted enabling the distinction of a group of occupations, which can be referred to as professions. An occupation can be considered a profession if it is conducted professionally through the provision of typical services, the activity is conducted to one's own account and—importantly—requires special qualifications or skills related to practicing the profession. Such activities should be conducted independently and personally, which does not, however, rule out the possibility of using the help of people who are subordinate to the person practicing the profession.[160]

712. When deciding not to define what other characteristics a profession has, the Polish lawmakers also assumed that they would arbitrarily list the professions which should be qualified for establishing a professional partnership. And so, only people who have the formal qualifications to practice a given profession can be partners in a professional partnership. The professions that authorize the establishment of a professional partnership are listed directly in the regulations. These are doctors, pharmacists, dentists, veterinarians, nurses, midwives, lawyers, architects, physiotherapists, construction engineers, statutory auditors, insurance brokers, laboratory analysts, tax advisers, securities brokers, investment advisers, accountants, notaries, legal advisers, patent attorneys, property valuers and sworn translators.[161]

713. As can be seen from the above list, the two main professional groups whose representatives can establish professional partnerships are legal practitioners and

160. Cf. J. Jacyszyn, *Wykonywanie wolnych zawodów w Polsce* [eng. *Practicing a Profession in Poland*], Warsaw 2004, pp. 44 et seq., U. Prominska (in:) *system prawa handlowego*, Volume 2A, p. 576 and A. Kidyba, *Prawo* ..., p. 308.
161. Article 88 CCCP.

people associated with health care. In addition, there are also people working in finance and accounting, as well as construction.

714. Articles of partnership must be concluded in writing to establish a professional partnership, and the partnership must be entered into the Register of Entrepreneurs of the National Court Register. The minimal content of the articles of partnership has been specified in the regulations. It includes the identification of the partners of the professional partnership, the forenames and surnames of the partners who have unlimited liability for the obligations of the professional partnership (if such a model of liability is chosen within the framework of the specific professional partnership), the definition of the profession exercised by the partners within the partnership, the forenames and surnames of the partners representing the partnership (if only some of the partners represent the partnership), the partnership's objects, the partnership's name and seat, the identification of the contributions made by each partner and their value, as well as the duration of the partnership if this is defined.[162]

715. As can be seen from the above, one of the required obligatory elements that must be specified in the articles of partnership is the indication of what profession is being practiced in that partnership. The specification of the profession should be unambiguous and precise.

716. The name of the professional partnership should contain a body consisting of the name of at least one partner and the obligatory marking of the partnership by placing two mandatory supplements in the name, the first being the term "*Spółka partnerska*" [Professional partnership] and the second is an indication of what profession is being practiced in the partnership.

717. Formally, according to Polish law, only professional partnerships have exclusive right to the terms "*i partner*" [and partner] or "*i partnerzy*" [and partners]. However, this does not prevent the widespread use of the term partner or partners by law firms in legal transactions which are introduced in any legal form other than a professional partnership.

718. The partnership is entered into the register of entrepreneurs of the National Court Register. The partnership is established upon entry into the register.

§3. Nature of the Unlimited Liability

719. The principles of liability of the partners for the partnership's liabilities constitute the main element that distinguishes this legal form from all other types of commercial law companies and partnerships.

162. Article 91 CCCP.

720. In principle, all partners are personally liable with their own property for the partnership's liabilities. However, the liability of the partners is ruled out in the case of the partnership's liabilities arising in connection with the other partners practicing the profession and in connection with omissions by people employed by the partnership on the basis of employment contracts or another legal relationship who were managed by another partner in the provision of services related to objects of the business.[163]

721. This means that the partners bear personal, unlimited liability with their own assets for the following liabilities of the partnership:

(1) liabilities arising in connection with them or people they manage making an error in their work;
(2) liabilities arising in connection with conducting business by a partnership which is not related to practicing a profession, e.g., for renting premises;
(3) the partnership's tax liabilities and liabilities from social security claims.

722. It should be emphasized that, in the model adopted in Polish law, the groups of liabilities of the individual partners, which are typical of professional partnerships around the world, are not permanent. The liability of the partner will always depend on whether he made a mistake through his own act or omission when practicing the profession resulting in the liability of the partnership, or whether such acts or omissions were committed by people he managed. Therefore, if, for example, Partner X is responsible for the fulfillment of orders for real estate transactions, but the given lease agreement was prepared by the Trainee Lawyer Z, who was supervised by Partner Y, then Partner Y will be responsible for the mistake made by the Trainee Lawyer.

§4. Contributions and Division of Profits

723. The partners participate in the partnership's profits and losses on the same terms as partners in a general partnership. I would like to refer the reader here to the relevant part of the study.

§5. Management

724. A professional partnership is the only legal form under Polish law in which the partners can decide for themselves which model of management they are adopting. A model can be chosen which is very similar to the model of managing a partnership which applies to a general partnership. However, it is also permissible to use a model that is typical of a limited liability company.

163. Article 95 CCCP.

725. In the former model, the professional partnership will be represented externally by one, several or all partners. In principle, each partner represents the partnership on his own. However, independent representation can be disabled and joint representation by more than one partner can be established in the articles of partnership. As in the case of a general partnership, any restrictions on the scope of representation, namely, for example, provisions from which it arises that a given partner cannot conclude contracts for the purchase or sale of real estate, or other such restrictions, would be ineffective.

726. A resolution depriving a partner of the right to represent the partnership may also be passed (for valid reasons) during the term of the partnership by a majority of three-quarters of the votes in the presence of two-thirds of the total number of partners.[164] A partner may also be deprived of the right to represent the partnership by court order.

727. If a model of management of the partnership is chosen that is similar to the one in force in a general partnership, each partner will also have the right and obligation to handle the partnership's affairs.

728. However, the partners may also accept a model for managing the partnership's affairs by the partnership's management board.[165] The ability to appoint a management board in a partnership was considered a revolutionary change by the representatives of the Polish legal doctrine. Until the CCCP was adopted, it was generally believed that the ability to appoint governing bodies structurally only suits companies, i.e., limited companies and joint-stock companies. However, when introducing a professional partnership into Polish law, it was decided that this partnership could have a management board if the partners so decide. In such a situation, the respective provisions regarding management in a limited liability company will apply. In practice, this means that the management board, if appointed, will represent the partnership externally and will handle its affairs. The right of representation of a member of the management board cannot be restricted with respect to third parties—this right encompasses all court and out-of-court activities related to the partnership. The method of representation of a partnership by a multiple-person management board, namely where each member of the management board can conclude agreements on behalf of the partnership and make declarations on his own or in cooperation with another member of the management board or a commercial representative, should be specified in the articles of partnership.

§6. Transferability of Partnership Interests

729. The transfer of a partner's shares to another person is possible on similar principles as in the case of a general partnership, provided however, that such a person is entitled to practice the profession that is practiced in the partnership. It should

164. Article 96 CCCP.
165. Article 97 CCCP.

be emphasized that this is not about the right to practice any of the professions listed in the regulations that enable the establishment of professional partnerships, but the specific profession that is practiced in the partnership. It should also be remembered that Polish law introduces restrictions on the ability of representatives of various professions to establish partnerships. For example, a common tactic in Germany of attorneys-at-law forming partnerships with notaries public is inadmissible in Poland because of the unambiguous wording of the law on the profession of attorney-at-law, which only allows an attorney-at-law to establish partnerships with other attorneys-at-law or legal counsels.

§7. Liquidation

730. In principle, partners may withdraw from the partnership, the partnership may be dissolved and the partnership may be liquidated according to the rules specified for a general partnership. However, a professional partnership has several specific solutions that only apply to that partnership.

731. The withdrawal of a partner from a professional partnership may be voluntary or obligatory. If a partner loses the right to practice a profession, he should withdraw from the partnership no later than at the end of the financial year in which he loses his right to practice the profession. This withdrawal is conducted by a written declaration addressed to the management board, if one has been appointed or to a partner authorized to represent the partnership, if there the partnership does not have a management board.[166] Therefore, Polish law actually allows for the possibility of being a partner in a partnership for a certain time, despite losing the right to practice the profession. However, this obviously does not mean consent for practicing a profession, but purely for remaining a partner in the partnership for a short time.[167]

732. A partnership may be dissolved for the reasons provided for in the articles of partnership, unanimously by all partners because of the declaration of the partnership's bankruptcy, the loss of the right of all partners to practice the profession or a final court decision.

733. Additionally, if only one partner remains in the partnership or if only one partner has the right to practice the profession related to the partnership's business, the partnership is dissolved no later than one year after the date of emergence of any of these events. This therefore means that a one-person partnership can exist for one year.[168]

734. The heirs of a partner of a professional partnership do not join the partnership in place of the deceased partner unless otherwise stipulated in the articles;

166. Article 100 CCCP.
167. Cf. A. Kidyba, *Prawo* …, p. 318.
168. Article 98 §2 CCCP.

although, in this situation, the heir may join the partnership only if he has the qualifications to practice the profession which was practiced in the partnership in which the partner was a partner.

§8. Taxation (In Brief)

735. A professional partnership is not a taxpayer of CIT. The same principles that apply to partners of a general partnership who are natural persons, which I discussed above, are applicable.

736. Furthermore, a limited partnership is also a remitter of VAT.

Chapter 4. Limited Joint-Stock Partnership

§1. To What Extent Does This Type Enjoy Legal Personality?

737. A limited joint-stock partnership has no legal personality under Polish law. However, it has legal identity, so it appears on its own behalf, concludes contracts, can sue and be sued, and has its own assets, which are separate from those of the partners.

§2. Establishment of the Partnership

738. A limited joint-stock partnership may be established in one of two ways.

739. First of all, a partnership may be established in the original way. The establishment of a partnership in this way requires the formation of a partnership, including the shareholders signing the articles of partnership, the partners subscribing for shares, the partners, both the shareholders and the general partners, making their contributions, and appointing a supervisory board if necessary to meet the requirements set out in the regulations. The last element required to establish the partnership will be the entry into the court register.

740. A limited joint-stock partnership's articles of partnership must be prepared in the form of a notarial deed. The articles of partnership must specify the name of the partnership and its seat, the partnership's objects, the surnames and forenames or the trade names of the general partners, the identification of the contributions made by each general partner and their value, the amount of share capital and the manner of its collection, the nominal value of the shares and their number, with an indication of whether shares are registered or bearer shares, the number of shares of the individual types and the related rights if shares of different types are to be introduced, surnames and forenames or firms (names) of the general partners and their registered offices, addresses or addresses for service or electronic delivery addresses, the principles of organization of the general meeting and the supervisory board (if the appointment of a supervisory board is necessary or planned) and the duration of the partnership if specified.[169]

741. The minimum amount of share capital in a limited joint-stock partnership is PLN 50,000; the shares in the limited joint-stock partnership are equal, of a nominal value of no less than PLN 0.01.

742. A supervisory board may be established in a limited joint-stock partnership, but this is obligatory if the number of shareholders exceeds twenty-five people.

169. Articles 130 and 131 CCCP.

743. A limited joint-stock partnership is established at the time of its entry into the court register.

744. The successive method consists of transforming another commercial company or a civil partnership into a limited joint-stock partnership.

§3. Nature of the Unlimited Liability

745. As mentioned above, there are two types of partners in a limited joint-stock partnership—general partners and shareholders.

746. The general partners are liable for the partnership's liabilities with all their property, jointly and severally with the other partners and the partnership, without any limitation. However, the shareholders are not liable for the partnership's liabilities.[170]

747. Therefore, in terms of liability for liabilities, general partners have an identical legal status to the partners of a general partnership or the general partners of a limited partnership. This liability is subsidiary to the partnership's liability, which means that the creditor of the limited joint-stock partnership may conduct enforcement on the general partner's property if enforcement against the partnership's assets proves ineffective. However, this does not prevent suing the general partner in parallel with the partnership.

748. The special rule applies, however, to general partners who are deprived of the right to represent the partnership by the court despite its objections. Such general partners are not liable for the partnership's liabilities.

§4. Contributions and Division of Profits

749. The provisions of Polish law do not contain any special regulations regarding the contributions and shares of equity of the general partners and shareholders in a limited joint-stock partnership. In this respect, similar provisions are applied to those that apply to the partners of a general partnership (in the case of a general partner) and in a joint-stock partnership (in the case of shareholders).

750. However, a special regulation regarding only limited joint-stock partnerships has been passed with regard to the share of the shareholders in the partnership's profit. The share of general partners and shareholders in the profit is primarily specified in the articles of the limited joint-stock partnership. Therefore, it is the partnership's founders who decide what kind of provisions on the distribution of

170. Article 135 CCCP.

profit they should enter into the articles of the limited joint-stock partnership. However, unless the articles provide a resolution on this, the general partners and shareholders participate in profits in proportion to the contribution made to the partnership. Additionally, the general partner handling the partnership's affairs and collecting a salary for this will not be entitled to a share of the profit to an extent corresponding to the contribution of his work to the partnership.[171] This latter rule was introduced so that the partner would not be paid twice for the same performance.

§5. Management

751. The limited joint-stock partnership is represented by the general partners, namely those partners of the limited joint-stock partnership who are personally liable for the partnership's liabilities.

752. It is, therefore, the general partners who actively handle and manage the partnership's activities.

753. In principle, each general partner may represent a limited joint-stock partnership on his own, although other solutions may be introduced into the articles of partnership. It is therefore possible, for example, to accept the principle that two general partners need to act jointly to represent the partnership and sign agreements on its behalf. The right of general partners to represent a limited joint-stock partnership encompasses all court and out-of-court activities of the partnership and cannot be limited with effect on third parties.

754. A general partner may be excluded from representing the partnership. First, the deprival of the right of representation may be applied by way of a resolution of the general meeting constituting an amendment to the articles of partnership and depriving the general partner of the right of representation. Such a resolution requires the consent of all the other general partners.[172]

755. However, in the case of objections from the general partner to whom the resolution applies, the right to represent the partnership may only be ruled out on the basis of a court decision, for valid reasons.

756. The internal relations of a limited joint-stock partnership are also handled by the general partners.

757. In principle, the shareholders do not have the right to represent the partnership or handle its affairs. They may, however, receive an authorization to represent the partnership as a commercial representative or a proxy. Importantly, Polish law

171. Article 147 CCCP.
172. Article 140 §3 CCCP.

contains a special provision that requires a shareholder acting on behalf of the partnership on the basis of a power of attorney that is granted to disclose the fact that he is acting as a proxy. If the shareholder fails to disclose this fact or performs activities on behalf of the partnership without authorization or if the scope of authorization is overstepped, then he is liable for the liability accepted on behalf of the partnership in the same way a general partner—he is liable for such liabilities without limitation, with all his property, jointly and severally with the other general partners and the partnership.[173]

§6. Transferability of Partnership Interests

758. Supplementing other rights that the rules regarding changes in the membership of the partners are different in the case of general partners and different in the case of shareholders also arises from the fact that a limited joint-stock partnership has two types of partners.

759. Shareholders can sell shares in a limited joint-stock partnership at any time. Therefore, changes in the composition of the shareholders may be frequent and are not subject to any restrictions. If a shareholder wants to leave the partnership, he does so by selling or otherwise disposing of the shares. The shareholder is not entitled to terminate the limited joint-stock articles of partnership.

760. However, general partners are subject to different regulations. A general partner may join a limited joint-stock partnership, but only if the articles so provided. The new general partner may be either a third party or an existing shareholder.[174]

761. Joining requires the consent of all existing general partners and the new submission by the general partner of a relevant statement on joining the partnership, agreeing to the wording of the articles of partnership and marking the contributions.

762. The general partner can also have the right to terminate the articles of association, provided that this is provided for in the articles of partnership themselves.

§7. Liquidation

763. The partnership is liquidated on the principles specified for a joint-stock company. In principle, the liquidators are those general partners who have the right to handle the affairs of the partnership.

173. Article 138 §2 CCCP.
174. Article 136 CCCP.

764. The reasons for the dissolution of a limited joint-stock partnership include the emergence of a statutory reason (specified in the articles of partnership), the passage of a resolution by the general meeting on the dissolution of the partnership, the declaration of the partnership's bankruptcy, death, the declaration of bankruptcy or the withdrawal of one general partner.

§8. Taxation (In Brief)

765. Although a limited joint-stock partnership is a partnership and has no legal personality, it has the status of a taxpayer of CIT. As in the case of companies, in addition to the partnership's income, the payment of a dividend to shareholders is also taxable.

766. Therefore, there is so-called double taxation in a limited joint-stock partnership—first, the partnership's income is taxed at the level of the partnership (CIT), and then, when the dividend is paid, it is taxed again, this time at the level of the partners. Partners of However, the partners of a limited joint-stock partnership can take advantage of tax preferences, as a result of which their profits are taxed once in practice.

767. A limited partnership is also a remitter of VAT.

Selected Bibliography

Allerhand M. *Kodeks handlowy*. Komentarz, reprint Bielsko-Biała, 1992.

Asłanowicz M. *Elementy konstrukcyjne osobowych spółek handlowych*. PS 2001, No. 5.

Asłanowicz M. *Pozycja prawna arbitra w arbitrażu handlowym*. Warsaw, 2015.

Asłanowicz M. *Sąd polubowny (arbitrażowy). Komentarz do art. 1154–1217 KPC*. Warsaw, 2017.

Banasiński C. & Jaroszyński K. M. *Komentarz do art. 18* [in:] C. Banasiński & K. M Jaroszyński. *Ustawa o gospodarce komunalnej Komentarz*. Warszawa, 2017.

Barański R. & Olejniczak A. *Fundacje i stowarzyszenia. Współpraca organizacji pozarządowych z administracją publiczną*. Warsaw, 2014.

Bieniak J., et al. *Kodeks spółek handlowych*. Komentarz, Warsaw, 2020.

Bilewska K. & Chłopecki A. *Prawo handlowe. Podręczniki Prawnicze*. Warsaw, 2019.

Binas P. *Prawo karne gospodarcze, red. R. Zawłocki, System Prawa Handlowego*. Vol. 10, Warszawa, 2018.

Błaszczyk P. *Ochrona wspólnika mniejszościowego spółki zależnej*. Warsaw, 2013.

Błaszczyk P. *Pojęcie grupy spółek na tle stosunku dominacji i zależności w kodeksie spółek handlowych*. PPH 2013, No. 7.

Brol J. & Safjan M. *Mandat a kadencja członka zarządu spółki z o.o. (art. 196 KH)*. PPH 1995, No. 11.

Bryłowski P. & Kidyba A. *Dopuszczalność świadczenia przez wspólników spółek jawnych usług doradczych na rzecz tych spółek w ramach prowadzonej przez wspólników działalności gospodarczej*. PPH 2011, No. 11.

Central Statistical Office, Warsaw, 2010.

Chłopecki A. *Prawna charakterystyka wezwań na sprzedaż i zamianę akcji*. [in:] *Prawo handlowe XXI w*.

Cyman D. & Zaręba-Cyman A. *Fundacje i stowarzyszenia prawny i podatkowy instruktaż funkcjonowania z wzorcową dokumentacją*. Gdańsk, 2013.

Declaration of respondents, Centre for Public Opinion Research of 2012.

Dolecki H. & Wiśniewski T. *Kodeks postępowania cywilnego*. Komentarz, Warsaw, 2012.

Dumkiewicz M. *Kodeks spółek handlowych*. Komentarz, Warsaw, 2020.

Frąckowiak J. *Instytucje prawa handlowego w kodeksie cywilnym*. Rej. 2003, No. 6.

Frąckowiak J., Kidyba A., Popiołek W., Pyzioł W. (ed.) & Witosz A., *Kodeks spółek handlowych. Komentarz*. Warsaw 2008.

Gasiński Ł. *Dopuszczalność wyłączenia prawa do zysku w statucie spółki akcyjnej.* PPH 2013, No. 10.
Gessel-Kalinowska vel Kalisz B. *Postępowanie przed sądem polubownym. Komentarz do Regulaminu Sądu Arbitrażowego przy Konfederacji Lewiatan.* Warsaw, 2016.
Goldiszewicz A. *Kilka uwag na temat możliwości rozwiązania spółki przy wykorzystaniu wzorca uchwały udostępnianego w systemie teleinformatycznym.* MoP 2016, No. 13.
Hadrowicz E. *Stowarzyszenie zwykłe w polskim systemie prawnym.* Toruń, 2014.
Jacyszyn J., Krześ S. & Marszałkowska-Krześ E., *Kodeks spółek handlowych. Komentarz. Orzecznictwo.* Warsaw, 2001.
Jacyszyn J. *Spółka partnerska według przepisów ustawy Kodeks spółek handlowych.* Bielsko-Biała 2001.
Jacyszyn J. *Wolne zawody w prawie handlowym.* GP 1999, Nos. 6–7.
Jacyszyn J. *Wykonywanie wolnych zawodów w Polsce.* Warsaw, 2004.
Jakubecki A. *Zdolność sądowa osobowych spółek handlowych a status ich wspólników w procesie cywilnym i egzekucji.* [in:] A. Nowicka (ed.). *Prawo prywatne czasu przemian. Księga pamiątkowa dedykowana Profesorowi Stanisławowi Sołtysińskiemu.* Poznań, 2005.
Jara Z. *Kodeks spółek handlowych.* Komentarz, Warsaw, 2020.
Kaliński J. *Prywatyzacja w Polsce po 1989 r.*
Kappes A. *Odpowiedzialność komandytariusza za zobowiązania spółki.* Kraków, 1997.
Kappes A. *Spółka komandytowa.* Warsaw, 1999.
Kappes A. *Wybrane zagadnienia odpowiedzialności za zobowiązania spółki komandytowej.* Pr. Spół. 1998, No. 10.
Katner W.J. & Fliszkiewicz K. *Łączenie się i inne rodzaje transformacji spółek handlowych ze szczególnym uwzględnieniem ochrony wierzycieli łączących się spółek kapitałowych (prawo polskie na tle prawa Unii Europejskiej).* [in:] Frąckowiak J. (ed.). *Kodeks spółek handlowych po dziesięciu latach.* Wrocław, 2013.
Katner W.J. *Pozakodeksowe uprzywilejowania akcji: konstrukcja "złotej akcji" Skarbu Państwa według ustawy z 2005 r.* PPH 2005, No. 12.
Katner W.J. *Prawo działalności gospodarczej.* Komentarz, Warsaw, 2003.
Kidyba A. (ed.). *Meritum. Prawo spółek.* Warsaw, 2016.
Kidyba A. (ed.). *Skarb państwa a działalność gospodarcza.* Warsaw, 2014.
Kidyba A. (ed.). *Spółka akcyjna.* Warsaw, 2014.
Kidyba A. (ed.). *Spółki Skarbu Państwa na rynku kapitałowym.* Warsaw, 2017.
Kidyba A. *Atypowe spółki handlowe.* Kraków, 2006.
Kidyba A. *Atypowe spółki handlowe.* Warsaw, 2011.
Kidyba A. *Komentarz aktualizowany do art. 1–300 Kodeksu spółek handlowych.* LEX, 2019.
Kidyba A. & Kopaczyńska-Pieczniak K. *Spółka kapitałowa bez kapitału zakładowego: głos w dyskusji nad projektem zmiany kodeksu spółek handlowych.* PPH 2011, No. 3.
Kidyba A. *Prawo handlowe.* Warsaw, 2019.
Kidyba A. *Spółka z ograniczoną odpowiedzialnością.* Komentarz, Warsaw, 2009.

Kidyba A. *Sukcesja, kontynuacja a może coś innego?*. MPH 2011, No. 1.
Kidyba A. *Ustawa o fundacjach. Prawo o stowarzyszeniach*. Warsaw, 1997.
Kidyba A. *Wybrane zagadnienia związane z likwidacją spółki z o.o.* MoP 2000, No. 13.
Koch A. & Napierała J. *Prawo spółek handlowych*. Warsaw, 2019.
Koralewski M. *Kodeks spółek handlowych 2020 z komentarzem*. Warsaw, 2020.
Krześniak E.J. *Odpowiedzialność partnerów za zobowiązania spółki partnerskiej*. PPH 2003, No. 3.
Krześniak E.J. *Rozwiązanie spółki partnerskiej*. PPH 2003, No. 7.
Krześniak E.J. *Spółka partnerska adwokatów (radców prawnych): wybrane zagadnienia*. Pal. 2002, Nos. 1–2.
Krześniak E.J. *Spółka partnerska ze szczególnym uwzględnieniem spółek adwokatów i radców prawnych*. Kraków, 2002.
Kułak K. *Stosunek członkostwa w zarządzie spółki kapitałowej*. Warsaw, 2015.
Kuniewicz Z. & Czepita A. *Aspekty wadliwości czynności prawnych spółki kapitałowej*. RPEiS 2002, sentence 3.
Kuniewicz Z. *Członek zarządu prokurentem w spółce kapitałowej*. PPH 2000, No. 5.
Leśniak M. *Internetowe wzorce umów handlowych spółek osobowych: konieczność czasów społeczeństwa informacyjnego*, PPH 2012, No. 9.
Leśniak M. *Normatywne wzorce umów spółek handlowych w prawie polskim*. Warsaw, 2017.
Leśniak M. *Spółka z o.o. zakładana za pomocą wzorca umowy: nowelizacja kodeksu spółek handlowych*. PPH 2011, No. 12.
Leśniak M. *Z problematyki prawnej pełnomocnictwa do reprezentowania spółki z ograniczoną odpowiedzialnością udzielonego na podstawie art. 210 § 1 k.s.h.* [in:] *Prawo handlowe XXI w.*
Litwińska M. *Spółka cywilna w świetle nowych regulacji prawnych Spółka Cywilna*. PPH 2001, No. 7.
Łaszczuk M. & J. Szpara. *Wybrane zagadnienia wykładni art. 230 KSH*. Pal. 2002, Nos. 7–8.
Oktaba R. *Prawo podatkowe*. Warszawa, 2019.
Opalski A. *Niektóre problemy wyboru grupowego członków rady nadzorczej*. PPH 2015, No. 2.
Pietrzykowski K. *Kodeks cywilny, red. K. Pietrzykowski*. vol. 2, Warszawa, 2018.
Prusek A. *Prywatyzacja polskiej gospodarki. Cele, programy i ocena ich rezultatów*. Kraków, 2005.
Rodzynkiewicz M. *Kodeks spółek handlowych*. Komentarz, Warsaw, 2013.
S. Włodyka [in:] S. Włodyka, *System prawa handlowego, tom pierwszy, Prawo handlowe: część ogólna*. Warsaw, 2009.
Sadlik R. *Umowa o pracę z członkiem zarządu spółki kapitałowej*. Pr. Spół. 2009, Nos. 7–8.
Smusz-Kulesza M. *Przedstawiciele w organach spółek powstałych w wyniku prywatyzacji i komercjalizacji przedsiębiorstw państwowych*. [in:] *Zbiorowe prawo pracowników do informacji*, Warszawa, 2012; https://sip.lex.pl/#/monograph/369

254414/171456?keyword=Zbiorowe%20prawo%20pracownik%C3%B3w%20do%20informacji%20Smusz-Kulesza&tocHit=1&cm=SREST (access: September 13, 2021).

Sobolewski P. & Tymoszko D. (eds), *Rozwój systemu finansowego w Polsce w 2008 r.* National Bank of Poland, Warsaw, 2009.

Sołtysiński S. (ed.). *System Prawa Prywatnego.* vol. 17A, Prawo spółek kapitałowych, Warsaw, 2010.

Sołtysiński S., et al. *Kodeks spółek handlowych.* Komentarz, vol. 1, Warsaw, 2001.

Statistical Yearbook 1990, Central Statistical Office, Warsaw, 1991.

Stefanicki R. *Transgraniczne łączenie się półek kapitałowych w świetle Dyrektywy Nr 2005/56 WE.* Rej. 2006, No. 5.

Suski P. *Stowarzyszenia i fundacje.* Warsaw, 2006.

Suski P. *Stowarzyszenia i fundacje.* Warsaw, 2008.

Szmitka S. *Specyfika cech prywatyzacji polskiej gospodarki początkowego okresu reform.*

Wierzbowski M. *Zależności oraz porozumienia akcjonariuszy w prawie o publicznym obrocie papierami wartościowymi.* PPH 2002, No. 5.

Witosz A. *Przekształcenia spółek w kodeksie spółek handlowych. Omówienia, wzory, przepisy, wskazówki praktyczne.* Bydgoszcz-Katowice, 2001.

Witosz A. *Restrukturyzacja spółek handlowych.* Bydgoszcz-Katowice, 2005.

Włodyka S. [in:] S. Włodyka. *System prawa handlowego, tom drugi, prawo spółek handlowych.* Warsaw, 2012.

Index

The numbers here refer to paragraph numbers.

Index

Index

www.ingramcontent.com/pod-product-compliance
Lightning Source LLC
Chambersburg PA
CBHW070252030525
26096CB00033B/1363
9789403532486